COUSINSGROUP

April 12,

IPO
PLAYBOOK

2012

Successful Integration management will ensure that the merger integration is structured effectively, planned properly and that progress is productively monitored. Merger integration when done right starts well before the deal is done.

Contents

Executive Summary

The conversion process involves detailed planning and participation by all areas of The company to effectively integrate the activities of the bank merging into an existing member bank, or creating a new member bank. The length of time required to integrate the acquired/merging bank will depend on complexity, including degree of standardization, number of charters, and to a lesser extent the size of the acquired bank. However, the general philosophy of the conversion process is to conduct activities in a manner that will optimize integration speed, maximize business objectives and manage impacts to customers, employees and other Company initiatives.

General Objectives

The objective of this Playbook is to describe the Bank integration methodology. It will describe the processes, phases and deliverables used at a general level to integrate the acquired bank. The integration is accomplished by breaking the project down into smaller work plan teams. This Playbook may be used by the newly assigned Specialty Coordinators, Team Members and staff of the bank to be integrated to better understand the process of the Project team.

Major Planning Assumption

The major planning assumption is that the merged bank's systems and products will be converted to The organization's current standards. Regional pricing and decision making authority will continue to apply to the extent possible under corporate policy standards.

Integration Management

Project planning is lead by the Integration Leader. Key strategic decisions will be made by an Executive Steering Committee, which includes heads of the major corporate business departments within The organization. Business lines may choose to assemble Task Forces representing the major areas of The organization's business units, systems operations and support functions to assist in the communication and issue resolution processes. The integration leader coordinates the steering committee roles and focuses on the cultural changes to the acquired bank. The IPO Manager, generally a member of the Administrative Services group of The company Bank heads the Integration team using the methodology described in this Playbook. The Project team includes a group of Specialty Coordinators who focus on conversion activities for their respective areas. The IPO manager will lead the coordinators and ensure activities are coordinated. Specialty Coordinators issues will direct issues and information to the related Business Line Managers. Specialty Coordinators will also lead a number of Team Leaders and teams within their assigned area of responsibility.

6

Integration Structure

Specialty Coordinators and Team Leaders are assigned to project tasks on a functional rather than a product line basis. For Example, Specialty Coordinators will be assigned for Operations, Systems, Training, Retail Banking, Commercial Banking, Trust Management, Support Services, etc. This philosophy was adopted to capitalize on the exchange of information, experience and ideas

Integration Project Phases

After the project team has been assembled, the integration will be guided by detailed Work Plans which will include phases described in this Playbook. Each phase has a specific objective and deliverables. Although all phases will be addressed, not all phases will be required under each Work Plan.

Employees of Team leaders within functional areas

It is the policy of XXX that impact to employees of XXX and the acquired bank(s) will be identified in the initial phases on integration. Human Resources Staff and Business Line management will communicate employee retention or outplacement programs, as well as any changes to benefit programs as early as possible in the integration process.

Customers

While the stated integration assumption is to convert all customers to XXX standards, complete analysis will identify all customer impacts, and resolve all issues that may arise out of the standardization process. As noted, regional pricing and decision making within the extent of corporate policy standards will continue to apply.

Communication

Communication is key to the successful integration for the three levels of communication: (1) Customer/other external parties, (2) Project, and (3) Organization. It is essential that all areas of the integration structure (Coordinators, Team Leaders, etc.) continually communicate their activities and progress to the other areas due to the significant amount of direct impacts they have on one another.

Quality communication includes many facets and people who are involved with and/or impacted by the integration project. Some examples of how communication efforts can be enhanced within and between project teams, employees, and management are as follows:

- Distribute project summaries, meeting minutes, issues, and assumptions and/or decision lists to Steering Committee members, Task Forces, Integration

7

Coordinator/Leader, Project IPO Manager, Project Coordinators, and Team Leaders, as appropriate.

- Conduct regular and on-going meetings with the various levels of bank management in XXX and the bank(s) being acquired, as well as conversion project leaders.
- Publish periodic newsletters to the employees regarding upcoming changes/events that will impact employees and/or customers of the bank(s).

The selection of a Communications Coordinator is important to accomplish the level and scope of communications required in integration projects. The communication efforts include internal communications to the bank's employees, and external communications to the bank's customers, and other interested parties.

<u>Methodology Exclusions</u>

Not included in this Playbook are the processes within the Mergers and Acquisitions Group, the Due Diligence Process, or the Legal Approval Process. This Playbook will discuss the importance of the project team reviewing the results of the Due Diligence Process and the communication with the Legal Department for understanding of timelines or issues within the Legal Approval process.

Project Roles and Responsibilities

Steering Committee

- Establishes the scope, business objectives and pacing assumptions
- Provides organizational definition
- Makes key strategic decisions on business line issues
- Ensures the availability and proper distribution of required resources
- Determines the state of the organization for conversion

Integration Leader (The Senior Vice President of Administrative Services will fill this position)

- Maintains Relationship between XXX and the acquired bank organization
- Clarifies the role of the Steering Committee and focuses on issues of cultural change and employee retention
- Drives the Steering Committee to quick decisions
- Implements directives of Executive Steering Committee to meet project goals/objectives
- Implements organizational and cultural change process within the new organization.
- Liaison to the organization experiencing the change in the following areas:

    o Objective Interpretation

    o Role Definition

    o Communication methods

    o Timeframes

    o Business Solution Alternatives

    o XXX Standard Strategic Priorities Process

IPO Manager

- Documents scope, strategy, objectives and assumptions
- Implements directives of the Executive Steering Committee.
- Establishes the integration project structure.

9

- Oversees day-to-day management of the project.
- Facilitates Project Plan development and staffing.
- Develops a high-level calendar of events
- Reviews Specialty Coordinator reporting
- Establishes a change control process and issue escalation process.
- Ensures project phases are scheduled and completed.
- Reports to the Steering Committee on project progress.
- Reports on project expense, issue resolution and change controls.

<u>Specialty Coordinator</u>

- Coordinate all conversion activities of a specific business, operations, or systems area of the bank.
- Lead the activities of specialized Team Leaders within their area to accomplish all deliverables.
- Interact with other Coordinators to ensure that issues are resolved and appropriate procedures are established.
- Submit monthly executive summary reporting.
- Provide summary Team budget management.
- Coordinate Team Leaders progress meetings.
- Resolve issues within and among teams. Escalates issues to the IPO Manager, as needed.
- Oversee development of Work Plan Summaries and detailed Work Plans.
- Ensure timely resolution of issues.
- Maintain continuous communication with IPO Manager and other Coordinators on all activities and status of project goals.
- Communicate frequently with Business Units being served and assesses "readiness" of Business Units for impact of resulting changes.
- Meet regularly with Key Stakeholders and representatives of management team of acquired bank(s), as necessary.
- Identify cross impact areas and coordinate the issues as necessary.
- Represent the following areas (however, IPO Manager will decide the structure of the Project Team for each project):
  - Computing and Communications
  - Internal and Customer Communications
  - Application Systems
  - Bank Operations
  - Customer Duplicate Account Numbers
  - Corporate Banking

- Trust Management
- Finance/Accounting/Controls
- Training Development & Delivery
- Staff Support Units
- Facilities
- Human Resources
- Audit
- Law
- Facilities/Purchasing
- Compliance
- Others, as required
- Specialized Coordinators: Integrated Test Coordinator, Implementation Coordinator, Post Support Coordinator

Team Leaders

- Assume responsibility for planning and implementation of assigned applications or functions.
- Develop Work Plan summary and detailed Work Plan.
- Direct Team members.
- Coordinate and communicate with other Coordinators and Team Leaders.
- Implement standard testing control procedures.
- Identify resources and coordinate with the resource management group.
- Conduct Team status meetings, as required.
- Produce product deliverables under each phase of the project in accordance with XXX standards.
- Obtain proper approvals.
- Assume responsibility for timely anticipation, escalation, and resolution of issues.
- Develop and track Team budgets.
- Provide monthly status reporting to Coordinators.
- Develop Test Plans.
- Develop Implementation Plans.
- Develop Post Support Plans.
- Develop Training Plans.
- Develop Customer Notification Plans.
- Develop and manage Change Control Requests.
- Coordinate with other Team leaders to manage dependencies.

Team Members

- Carry out tasks as assigned by Team Leader.
- Provide reporting as required.

Business Line Management /Task Force

- Task forces are assembled at the discretion of the Business Unit Heads, and will include Business Line decision makers and Team Leaders. Task forces may be limited to the Team members.
- Members may participate from XXX as well as bank(s) being acquired.
- Take direction from early decisions/assumptions established by Executive Steering Committee and Integration Leader.
- Identify issues relative to the specific area represented, and impacts to the functions of this area;
  - Assist in identification of impacts of these issues to other areas;
  - Establish resolution of issues through Project Coordinators.
- Communicate issues/assumptions/decisions to other Task Forces and Project Coordinators.

Best Practices

The Playbook contains several best practices that are specific and practical steps to support the conversion process.

<u>General</u>

Conduct Formal education for all team members regarding processes and deliverables throughout all phases of the integration.

Develop a financial tracking plan that includes all areas of the organization. Establish a Financial specialty coordinator to support this need.

Communication strategy and plans should provide face-to-face forums to educate both organizations as to the integration objectives, key assumptions and cultural expectations.

<u>Planning</u>

Use a comprehensive checklist that includes all business units when creating the budget and afterwards.

Provide a formal turnover venue from the Due Diligence team to the integration team.

Conduct a risk assessment that focuses on systems, products and operational processes for key businesses and business customers with the intent of identifying and implementing effective contingency plans that are designed to mitigate significant integration risks.

Establish an Integration Program Office (IPO) and educate active participants in their roles and responsibilities.

<u>Discovery & Analysis</u>

Each business and operations area must conduct a formal review of their workflow mapping analysis.

Need to establish "mandatory" and "nice to have" criteria for enhancements when confirming both business and technical requirements.

Develop a decision hierarchy to identify who is responsible to create and approve business requirements.

Standardize business requirements template and educate the business units.

Allocate and commit the appropriate resources with the right skill sets and knowledge.

Formulate a focus group that represents each business unit across the organization that would communicate to external customers and provide a more consolidated contact.

The two-step approach evaluation process should be addressed in the Planning phase of integration.(need to assess relevance and value add)

Develop an organization wide standard contingency plan template using the LDRPS Contingency Planning Platform tool. Perform Risk Assessments to each key business area identified and let the outcome drive what contingency plans should be created.

Readiness

Engineer the process for what is tested including appropriate test plans & scripts, checklists and signoffs of successful results with all technologies.

Provide a specialty coordinator who can identify the strategy, monitor its progress and regularly report to the integration team. (Value)

Allocate appropriate level of resources and time in the plan to execute end-to-end testing of critical operational processes and system applications prior to integration.

Define the training requirements and the curriculum and examine best practices for the training development. Align the acquired organization with the acquiring organizations so they together can determine the appropriate level of training. Document and effectively track progress based on the plan throughout integration.

Training

Assurance of consistency, quality and comprehension within the training programs

Provide employees with the opportunity to practice; simulate "real life" situations in which to apply learning.

Provide "hands on" experience using reference materials

Train in "stages" such that most critical pieces of training are closest to conversion date and each piece reinforces the previous.

14

Conduct pilot training sessions to provide opportunity for evaluation prior to full rollout of training sessions.

Conduct management orientation sessions to obtain support and inform of specific roles/responsibilities of all involved.

Conduct follow-up evaluations of all sessions to make improvements to training and to provide additional support/training to employees as needed.

Reinforce/Evaluate comprehension of information on which employees are trained.

Management is responsible for ensuring employees are trained and comprehend what they have learned.

Implementation

Establish "what should be in the organization wide detail plan" and "what tools should be used to track the weekend activities" and communicate/educate the team providing this information.

Use a progress reporting tool that clearly communicates the weekend plan progress and problem reporting functions and can be accessed internally and remotely, so interested participants can receive up to the minute status of progress.

PROJECT PHASES

After the Due Diligence process and a decision has been made to process with the integration, an Integration Leader, IPO Manager and a steering Committee will be selected to direct the process. The Integration Program Office (IPO) will be established.

The Integration program is divided into the following phases:

- Due Diligence
- Phase 1   Planning
- Phase 2   Discovery and analysis
- Phase 3   Readiness
- Phase 4   Implementation
- Phase 5   Post Implementation
- Phase 6   Debriefing/Review

See Integration Project Milestone and dependencies Chart

These phases are not always performed sequentially. Some phases may begin while others are in progress. Each Coordinator or Team Leader may not perform in each phase, however all phases must be performed by some Team Leaders to accomplish a successful integration. Each phase will outline the roles of required participants.

DUE DILIGENCE

Corporate Planning and Development is responsible for identifying potential acquisition targets, reviewing and analyzing those targets, directing the due diligence process, gaining executive approval for making an offer, working with the Legal Department and the Regulatory agencies and negotiating with the target company's management or broker. A Due Diligence Team is comprised of appropriate XXX business line and staff due diligence representatives. The Due Diligence Team, working in complete confidentiality, will then be responsible to complete an analysis. Each team member works with their senior management to present findings to Corporate Planning. The deliverables will then be shared with the IPO Manager upon signing of the contract.

The Due Diligence Team will engage in a period of data gathering and from analysis of that data, will produce the list of deliverables. Below are the general categories of data that are requested from the target in the Due Diligence Process:

- Organizational Structure
- Data Centers, Branches, Commercial Offices, etc
- Organization Charts
- Staffing Levels
- Fixed asset inventory
- Budgets-income, expense capital
- Contracts in excess of $15M
- Background of management and key employees
- Current key initiatives/projects
- Culture/atmosphere/ turnover
- Technology Platforms
- Service Bureau services provided
- Fee income services provided
- Data Center information
- Distributed Systems
- Data Security system
- Disaster Recovery capabilities
- List of products and services and major features
- Productivity / quality reports

Upon completion of the contract, the Integration Steering Committee, Integration Leader and IPO Manager will assemble and review assumptions. In order to avoid redundancy, the data and deliverables from the Due Diligence phase will then be shared with the appropriate Integration Project Specialty coordinators and will serve as a basis for the major integration assumptions.

Insert Milestone Chart

PHASE 1- PLANNING

Purpose

The main purpose of the planning phase is to determine project structure, objectives, scope, integration approach, assumptions, calendar, and preliminary issues. After the due diligence process and a decision has been made to proceed with the integration, an Integration Leader, an IPO Manager, and a Steering Committee will be selected to direct the process. The Integration Leader will ensure implementation of Executive Steering Committee Decisions, and act as the communication link between the Steering Committee, Business Unit Members, IPO Manager, and the Project Teams.

IPO Manager/Steering Committee Role

Participants

With the assistance of the Integration Leader, the Steering Committee will establish integration strategy, scope, and objectives. The IPO Manager will assume the day-to-day management of the project, and must document the decisions of the Steering Committee and Integration Leader.

The IPO Manager and Integration Leader will work with the Steering Committee to establish the project structure and work to fill the desired positions for Project Coordinators.

IPO Manager Deliverables

In preparation for the Kickoff Meeting with the Project Coordinators, the IPO Manager must prepare or document the following deliverables:

- Organizational Definition – Local, Regional and Centralized Activities; Pricing Regions
- Preliminary Major Planning Assumptions
- Integration Objectives
    - o In Scope/Out of Scope
    - o Merger Date
    - o Structure
    - o Name
    - o Standards: Products and Operations
    - o Processing Centers

- o Outsource/Vendor arrangements
- o History/Retrieval Conversion
- o Impact to current projects
- Preliminary Milestone Document (Project Calendar/Implementation Plan)
- Roles and Responsibilities Document (Administrative & Coordinators)
- Preliminary Issues List
- Budget assumptions from due diligence (for further development)
- Due Diligence Information Distribution, including organizational definition
- Meeting schedule, locations, and format
- Expense Reimbursement Guidelines
- Change Control Process Guidelines
- Budget Tracking Process Guidelines

Examples of early action items to be assigned:

- Coordinator Selection/Bank Target Partners
- Establish Communication links (mail, voicemail, shared drive, e-mail, video conference, etc.)
- Plan for Employee and Customer Communication
- Develop a communications strategy for the bank to be acquired
- Schedule Overview Sessions
- Determine Facilities and Capacity Issues
- Determine Communications Coordinator
- Determine Budget Tracking Coordinator
- Determine Change Control Coordinator
- Determine retention and stay-bonus strategies
- Resource Requirements- Resource Management Involvement
- Schedule discovery visit to bank
- Validate due diligence cost projections
- Evaluate Systems Support Strategies
- Schedule Process Overview sessions with key partners

Specialty Coordinator Selection

Participants

The IPO Manager works with the Integration Leader and the Steering Committee to select the appropriate personnel from the Service Company , the Systems Group, the Operations Group, the Business Lines, the Support Services Groups, or from outside the bank. The selected staff must have strong organizational and communication skills.

20

The Managers of the selected staff must recognize the critical nature of the project, and be willing to dedicate their best resources to accomplishing the objectives of the acquisition. Coordinators are normally dedication 100% of their time to the project.

Retail

Directs/oversees activities for the following areas:

- Product/Pricing
- Customer Notifications
- Forms
- Insurance
- Branch Operations/Administration
- Retail Credit Administration
- Consumer Loan Services
- Branch Set Up (forms, equipment, etc.)
- Retail Training
- Customer Service/Call Center
- Credit Card

Training

- Orientation/Overview of training that will take place for each major area of the bank
- Coordinates training activities
- Coordinates/develops training programs
- Coordinates training facilities/equipment
- Performs quality review of training activities
- Evaluates effectiveness of training after conversion effort has been completed
- Consults with Coordinators
- Reviews impact analysis documentation

Forms

- Identifies forms requiring/creation based on interface with various areas of the bank
- Coordinates production of all forms needed
- Coordinates ordering of forms, stationery, paper and related supplies
- Coordinates distribution of forms and supplies to appropriate areas
- Coordinates destruction of obsolete forms and supplies

Customer and Internal Notifications

- Coordinates and manages internal communications functions (i.e. newsletters, announcements, etc.) to employees
- Coordinates and manages external communications (i.e. customer notifications, press releases, etc.)

Business Banking

Directs/oversees the following instructions:

- Product/Pricing
- Customer Notifications
- Corporate Training
- Credit Administration
- International Sales and Operations
- Cash Management Products and Product Strategy
- Documentation
- Syndications
- Commercial Finance
- Leasing
- Loan Review
- Secured Credit
- Corporate Services Support
- Commercial Lending

Systems

May direct/oversee the following systems conversion activities:

- CORE/Non-CORE Systems
- Independent Systems
- Account Renumbering
- Vendor Liaison
- Database Merger (if applicable)
- Conversion Balancing/Controls
- Data Warehousing

Operations

Directs and oversees the following areas in conversion activities:

- Deposit Operations
- Cash Management Operations
- Item Processing Operations, including item capture, Statement Sorting, Float, and associated hardware and software (i.e. sorters, reject repair, etc.)
- Business Loan Operations
- Trust and Financial Operations
- Operations Equipment
- Operations Training
- Special Business Units
- Central Proof (Financial)

Data Center and Communications

Directs and oversees activities related to all data center functions as follows:

- Voice/Data/Video/Communications Services
- Client Services
- LAN/WAN Servers, Desktop Computing
- Support Center
- Technical Services
- Performance/Capacity, Data Storage/Software Distribution, Data Management, Operating
- Systems
- Data Center Operations
- Facilities, Print/Fiche, Scheduling
- Data Security
- Closure of acquired/merging bank(s) Data Center (if applicable)

Mortgage

Directs and oversees activities related to mortgage originations, underwriting, funding, closing, processing, and servicing:

Finance

23

- Directs and oversees activities related to finance:
- Corporate Accounting- Conversion and Interface
- General Ledger- Accounting, Regulatory Reporting, Bank Reconciliation,
- Budget- Organization, Allocations, Analysis/Planning
- Management Reporting- Production, Costing,
- Project Impact, Reporting
- Bank Reporting- Customer impacts, Reporting Inventory, Report Migration
- Treasury- XXX Reporting, Tax, Insurance, Investor Relations, E&Y

Support Services

Depending on the size of the acquisition, some of the following areas may have their own coordinator:

- Human Resources
- Audit
- Corporate Purchasing/Warehouse
- Compliance/Risk Management
- Legal Department
- Community Development
- Strategic Planning
- Mergers and Acquisitions
- Corporate Communications
- Bank Security
- Facilities

Legal

Approval and related legal issues (i.e. name changes)

Communications

Internal and external communications

Special Coordinators

- Integrated Test Coordinator
- Implementation Coordinator
- Post Support Coordinator

Other Business Coordinators

Coordinators may be assigned to other Business Units, as required.

Each Coordinator has a team of Team Leaders working with them on specific tasks to accomplish the many activities within their area. Therefore, a Team Leader is a tactical project manager, reporting to the respective Coordinator on their activities.

IPO Manager Kickoff with Specialty Coordinators

A "Kickoff" meeting is the first meeting of the project team within each layer of the project structure. At each meeting, all of the information known to date, and relating to project objectives, is shared with the teams.

At the IPO Manager's meeting with the assigned Specialty Coordinators, the following information from the Integration Leader Planning Phase will be discussed:

- Organizational Definition- Local, Regional and Centralized Activities
- Product to system map; Pricing Regions
- Preliminary Major Planning Assumptions
- Integration Objectives and Approach
    - In Scope/Out of Scope
    - Merger Date
    - Structure
    - Name
    - Standards: Products and Operations
    - Processing Centers
    - Outsource/Vendor arrangements
    - History/Retrieval Conversion
    - Impact to current projects
- Preliminary Milestone Document (Project Calendar/Implementation Plan)
- Roles and Responsibilities Document (Administrative & Coordinators)
- Preliminary Issues List
- Due Diligence Information Distribution, including organizational definition
- Schedule of Process Overview sessions with key partners
- Legal Approval Discussion

- Meeting schedule, locations, and format
- Expense Reimbursement Guidelines
- Change Control Process Guidelines/Name of CC Manager
- Budget assumptions from due diligence (for further development)
- Budget Tracking Process Guidelines/Name of Budget Manager
- Project Numbering Information
- Discussion of Retention/Stay Bonus Strategies
- Vacation Policy Discussion

Update of the following Early Action Items to be assigned:

- Establish Communication links (mail, voicemail, shared drive, e-mail, video conference, etc)
- Plan for Employee and Customer Communication
- Develop a communications strategy for the bank to be acquired
- Determine Facilities and Capacity Issues
- Evaluate Systems Support Strategies

Discussion of deliverables/dates needed from Coordinators:

- Roles and responsibilities documents for Team Leaders
- Additions to Assumptions List
- Additions to Issues List

Discussion on selection of Team Leaders and the role of the Resource Management Group

Discussion of deliverables/dates from Team Leaders:

- Roles and responsibilities documents for Team Members
- Additions to Assumptions List
- Additions to Issues List
- Work Plan Summary
- Detailed Work Plan
- Budget Plan (Revision of Due Diligence Assumptions)
- Change Control Requests

Team Leader Selection/ Specialty Coordinator Kickoff

Each Coordinator will determine the number and responsibilities of Team Leaders under their direction. The Coordinator will request Service Company resources, as needed.

The requests should state the skills required, and the percent of Team Leader's time that is required for the project. Resource Management will secure and assign resources to each project plan. Team Leaders are generally 100% of their time dedicated to the project, and will assign detailed tasks to team members.

After staff members have been notified of their assignment to the project, a Kickoff Meeting will be held with the Team Leaders. All information obtained from the IPO Manager and further discussions about the project known to date will be shared with the Team Leaders. A recap of this information is:

- Organizational Definition- Local, Regional and Centralized Activities
- Pricing Regions
- Preliminary Major Planning Assumptions
- Integration Objectives
    - In Scope/Out of Scope
    - Merger Date
    - Structure
    - Name
    - Standards: Products and Operations
    - Processing Centers
    - Outsource/Vendor arrangements
    - History/Retrieval Conversion
    - Impact to current projects
- Preliminary Milestone Document (Project Calendar/Implementation Plan)
- Roles and Responsibilities Document (Administrative & Coordinators)
- Preliminary Issues List
- Due Diligence Information Distribution, including organizational definition
- Schedule of Process Overview sessions with key partners
- Legal Approval Discussion
- Meeting schedule, locations, and format
- Expense Reimbursement Guidelines
- Change Control Process Guidelines/Name of CC Manager
- Budget assumptions from due diligence (for further development)
- Budget Tracking Process Guidelines/Name of Budget Manager
- Project Numbering Information
- Discussion of Retention/Stay Bonus Strategies
- Vacation Policy Discussion
- In addition to setting up further meeting schedules, a discussion will be held regarding the Communication Plan for each team

COUSINSGROUP

- Discussion of deliverables/dates needed from Team Leaders:
  - Roles and responsibilities documents from Team Members
  - Additions to Assumptions List
  - Additions to Issues List
  - Work Plan Summary
  - Detailed Work Plan
  - Budget Plan (Revision of Due Diligence Assumptions)
  - Change Control Requests
  - Monthly executive summary reporting

Team Selection / Team Leader Kickoff*

Team selection process and kickoff meetings will follow the same format as the IPO Manager/Specialty Coordinator Kickoff.) Team meetings will be scheduled by the Team Leader. Team Members will be involved in the creation of the deliverables listed in the previous section (IPO Manager/Specialty Coordinator Kickoff).

Internal & External Communication Plan

A Communications Coordinator and Communications Team will be named for each Integration Projects, in most cases from the marketing area of the Bank. Every Team Leader will be responsible for communicating with the Communications Coordinator or Team representative with regard to the changes that affect the external bank customers. The Communications team will develop appropriate internal and external communications to notify these customers segments. (See the Communications Plan Deliverables- Phase 4 of this manual for further detail.)

Deliverables

Product Overview Sessions

Responsibility	BUSINESS LINE PRODUCT MANAGERS
Description	This informative session(s) is held prior to Project mapping meetings. These sessions are held at the discretion of each business area. This overview session provides the bank to be integrated with a glimpse of what projects and systems will be available through XXX Bank.
Audience	This overview presentation is attended by all individuals involved in the conversion process within the specified product areas. It may

28

also include representatives from management from both banks. The sessions will not include the level of product features covered in the product mapping sessions.

Major Assumptions List

Responsibility	IPO MANAGER, PROJECT COORDINATORS, TEAM LEADERS
Distribution	The list is originated and kept by the IPO Manager, and further defined by the Project Coordinators and Team Leaders as major issues are resolved as decisions. As Assumptions are added to the list, it is the responsibility of the project teams to review each new assumption, and challenge or approve the assumption within 30 days. Verification should occur prior to moving an assumption to a decision. Written approval documentation should support decisions made.
Description	Short statements are made in list format identifying the major planning assumptions of the integration.
Example	1 XXXXXX Corporation will be merged, converted, and consolidated into XXX during the XXXX quarter of 20XX. 2. The Organizational Definition will be validated by the XXXX Executive Steering Committee. 3. The new bank will have XX pricing regions. Community Banks will report to the head of Retail Banking. 4. The name of the bank will be changed to XXXXX effective with the systems and operations conversion. 5. All XXX systems will convert to XXX Standard Systems. No enhancements will be made to the current core systems prior to conversions. 6. XXX standard products and operations will be implemented for XXXX. 7. XXX standard forms, reports, screens, procedures, and training delivery systems will be implemented. 8. A regional processing center will be established XXXXX. 9. Current Service Company functions will be centralized for XXXX. 10. Wire Transfer and ACH will be consolidated to the Lavonia Regional Center.

11. Account Analysis will be consolidated into the Lavonia Regional Center.

12. ATM operations will be consolidated into the Lavonia Regional Center.

Responsibilities Documents

- Contact List
- Responsibility Chart

Responsibility   IPO MANAGER, COORDINATORS, TEAM LEADERS

Description   The IPO Manager, Coordinators, and Team Leaders will create two types of documents: Contact List, and a Responsibilities Chart.

The Contact List should include:
Name
Project Title (i.e. Retail Coordinator)
Address/Locator
Work/Home Telephone number
Voicemail number
Fax number
Pager number
Cell phone number

The Responsibilities Chart is done in an organizational chart format, and will include the list of names, project titles, and areas of responsibilities. Each person responsible for creating this document would list the names and responsibilities of staff reporting to them. The chart should also note areas of responsibilities that maybe assigned to other coordinators.

Project Milestones (aka Project Event Calendar)

Responsibility   IPO MANAGER, PROJECT COORDINATORS, TEAM LEADERS

Description   Project milestone dates are established for each major high level activity that is part of the overall project plan; these dates represent the time frames in which these activities will be accomplished to keep the project on schedule.

30

Team leaders create their Task plan Summaries and ultimately their Detailed Task plans based upon these dates with all required tasks to achieve milestone completion by targeted date.

Other areas of the project including their support/related activities as necessary around these milestone dates (for example, based on training milestones the Training Specialty coordinator works with the Retail Specialty coordinator and Training Team leader to provide training facilities, equipment, etc.)

Format

Milestone Document may take the format of a spreadsheet or Gantt Chart showing the Milestone Title and the months that the associated tasks should begin and end.

Header information	Spreadsheet
Document Title	Milestone Title
Prepared By	Months
Original Date	
Revised Date	

Example:

XXXX Integration Project
Milestone Document Example
(Example)

Prepared By:
Date:
Revised Date:

Month Start Date	Milestone	Planned Completion Date	Revised Completion Date	Actual Completion Date
September	Director Planning Phase			
09/01/20XX				
October				
November				
December				

31

Work Plan Summary

Responsibility   COORDINATORS, TEAM LEADERS

Distribution   IPO Manager, Project Coordinators, all affected Team Leaders, Team Members

Description   The Work Plan Summary is a narrative document that defines the scope of conversion activities for a particular Work Plan. Documents that can be used to create the Work Plan Summary, if available are:

- Questionnaires
- Product Lists from the Converting Bank
- Project Organizational charts
- Major Milestones
- Planning Guidelines
- Account Information: types, volumes, etc.

Upon completion of all Work Plan summaries, those areas not covered and those areas overlapping in two or more areas must be addressed by the IPO Manager. The Summary is also used to build a detailed task plan.

Format   A Work Plan Summary addresses the topics outlined below:

Heading
- Work Plan Name
- Team Leader
- Date Created
- Team Leader Contact Information
- Project Number (Systems & Operations only)

Work Plan Description
Denotes the application/process being converted For example:
- Consumer Lending Operations

- DDA Systems Conversion

Project Objective

A broad/high level statement of the activities for which the Team Leader will be responsible for during the entire integration project.

Specific Responsibilities

A listing of specific conversion project activities for which the Team Leaders will be responsible. The specific tasks listed in this portion of the Work Plan Summary will be the foundation from which the detailed Project Work Plan is developed.

Implementation Approach/Interdependencies

- A listing of specific conversion approaches to be used in order to complete the conversion process.
- A listing of project teams with whom there is a dependency in order to complete the conversion project using the approaches listed above.
- The listing of implementation approaches and interdependencies will have a direct impact on the development of the detailed Project Work Plan.

Detailed Work Plan

Responsibility   Team Leader

Distribution   IPO Manager, Group Coordinator, other affected Coordinators, affected Team Leader.

Description   The Detailed Work Plan is a comprehensive listing of tasks which are required to complete the conversion process defined by the Work Plan Summary. Samples of detailed Work Plans are available from the last XXX conversion. The tasks should be listed in phases and sub-phases. The detailed Work Plan is formatted to exhibit the following items:

- Task Number: a unique number for each task in the Detailed Work Plan. Sub-phases of each task maybe labeled with decimal points.

COUSINSGROUP

- Task/Action Required: a narrative of the activities required to complete a specific project task. Tasks will follow the Project Phase/Deliverables items.
- Resource: a listing of individual(s) responsible for the completion of a task.
- Start Date: the date activities are scheduled to conclude for a specific project task.
- End Date: the date activities are scheduled to conclude for a specific project task.
- Status: current status for a specific project task:
  - Inactive
  - Active
  - complete

Planning   Plan/Supervise/Coordinate

- Includes a variety of ongoing project tasks for which the Team Leader is responsible:
  - Provide direction to team members.
  - Attend general conversion related meetings.
  - Finalize on-site dates and resources.
  - XXX Product Standards documentation.
  - Project status reporting plan.
  - Project Controls, Training, Testing, Conversion, Post-Implementation Support Strategy Development.
  - Interface/Systems Identification.
  - Maintenance/distribution of the project's Assumptions/issues/Decisions document.
- Draft a Detailed Work Plan.
- Identify/obtain required resources.
- Conduct a project Kickoff Meeting.

Discovery & Analysis   Product Mapping

- Map the converting bank's products to XXX's product base. Review and obtain approval.
- Draft and distribute a product mapping document reflecting how the products have been mapped, including impacts lists, customer notification, revenue, process, etc.
- Incorporate unresolved mapping issues into the project's Issues List document

34

- Gather product volume counts

Data Base Mapping

- Attend Data Base Mapping session conducted by the systems Team Leader.
- Incorporate unresolved mapping issues into the project's Issues List document.
- Document table information: mapping i.e., officer numbers, region numbers, division numbers, service units, other code tables.
- Create financial hierarchy map. Obtain proper approval.
- Determine report requirements, distribution plan, general report setup list, document report differences, and identify courier schedules. Obtain proper approval.
- Develop account renumbering plan and documentation.
- Document systems Requirements and specifications.

Customer Impacts

- Identify customer notification requirements during Product and Data Base Mapping sessions.
- Document open issues and legal constraints.
- Resolve and document open issues.

Impact analysis & Resolution

- Complete a functional organization chart for the converting bank if required.
- Interview appropriate departmental workstations.
- Identify operational exceptions and impacts.
- Identify policy differences and impacts.
- Draft and distribute an Operations Impacts Document. Include interface impacts.
- Conduct an Impacts Review meeting if required
- Assign and resolve impact differences and issues.
- Forms and Reports:
  - Identify forms to be replaced.
  - Identify post conversion reports distribution.

Readiness

Procedures Development
- Develop required Interim Procedures.
- Modify required Existing Procedures.
- Develop required New Procedures.
- Obtain management approval for all procedures.
- Distribute all required procedures.

Application Set up
- Define DASD Requirements.
- Review & modify merge procedures- balancing/validation.
- Modify job production streams.
- Setup Delivery.
- Setup Test Files and Test JCL.

Department Set-up
- Facilities
  - Identify required changes to facilities due to additional staffing, file space, processing equipment, etc.
  - Scheduling of facilities changes.
  - Complete department breakdown, as necessary.
- Equipment
  - Identification of equipment needs or the need to dispose of equipment.
  - Order new required equipment.
  - Install/test new equipment.
- Forms
  - Identify forms required. (XXX standard forms)
  - Order and receive required forms.
  - Schedule placement of new forms.
  - Schedule destruction of old forms.
- Personnel/Staffing
  - Identify additional staffing requirements.
  - Identify staff reorganization requirements.
  - Obtain approval for addition or reorganized staffing.
  - Implement new or reorganized staff.
- Logon IDs
  - Identify individuals requiring access (add logon IDs) to XXX systems.

36

- o Identify level of access required: Inquiry-Data Entry-Supervisor.
  - o Process appropriate logon ID request forms and obtain logon IDs.
- Files Transport
  - o Identify all files to be moved to centralized XXX process sites: Operations Centers.
  - o Identify procedures and schedule for the transport of all files.
  - o Transport files.
- Develop a Critical Success Factors Document
  - o Document all required pre-conversion maintenance.
  - o Document all required post conversion maintenance.

Training

- Review Impact Analysis and Product Mapping documentation to assist in program development.
- Assist Training Team Leader and Training Coordinator in developing an XXX training program. Include training materials, dates, locations, samples, reports, trainee requirements, trainee notification, scheduling, and facilities.
- Schedule centralized G.L. reconciliation training.
- Document training questions and issues.
- Identify method of training, and obtain resources.

Testing

- Identify a Testing Coordinator to monitor operations testing tasks and interface with the Systems Conversion Team.
- Review conversion balancing procedures for testing and conversion.
- Code Programs- hierarchy changes, security changes, interface changes, control file changes, application data, sort pattern changes, table changes.
- Unit Test Merge Process.
- Execute Unit Testing, including custom code changes.
- Prepare integrated test plan.
- Develop User Validation test criteria.
- Develop test cases and/or test data.
- Conduct System Testing/balancing/verification.

- Make corrections to JCL, Programs, etc.
- Develop test plan for user verification of interfaces for Integrated Testing.
- Execute/complete merge process.
- Balancing/Verification- Integrated Test.
- User validation of output/interface files.
- Prepare Test Results packet.
- Review with member banks.
- Conduct Dry Run Test- execute merge, balancing/verification.

Implementation

Implementation Plan

- Identify tasks required for conversion. This plan covers a period of time from one month prior to conversion through scheduled conversion tasks.
- Conduct Implementation Plan Review Meeting to verify all team members know their assigned implementation tasks and time frames.
- Identify cross impacts.
- Identify conversion staffing requirements.
- Identify contingency plans.
- Indentify control criteria.
- Draft/distribute On-site/On-call conversion matrix.
- Define and document contingency/backup procedures in the event of a failed conversion.
- Hold Technical and Operational Last Day Processing Meetings.
- Execute Bank Merge.
- Balance and Verify. Obtain conversion signoff.

Post Support

Post Implementation

- Develop and implement a post-implementation support plan including onsite assistance and/or a branch Helpline.
- Identify key monitoring criteria.
- Develop and maintain a Problem Log, prioritize, assign and resolve problems.
- Develop and update phone and meeting distribution plan.
- Participate in post-implementation support meetings as required.

- Address retraining.
- Review and schedule post conversion items.
- Hold status meetings.
- Assemble project repositories.
- Document strengths/weaknesses. Modify final conversion plans to address problem.

Example:

Project Name
Detailed Work Plan
(*Example*)

Work Plan Name:
Team Leader:
Contact Information:
Team Members:

Task No.	Task/Action Required	Assigned To:	Start Date:	End Date:	Status	Dependency (Task No.)
1.0						
1.01						
1.02						
1.03						

Work Budget Plan

Responsibility   ALL TEAM LEADERS, ALL COORDINATORS

Description   Each Team Leader will prepare an initial project budget for all participants in their work plan, according to administrative directives supplied at the beginning of the project. See "Project Budget Tracking" in the Standard XXX Processes Section of this manual. (Need to have Reference)

Customer Notification Plan/Internal Notification Matrix

Responsibility   PROJECT COMMUNICATIONS COORDINATOR with assistance from TEAM LEADERS from BUSINESS LINES

Description

The following are key steps to developing an effective communication plan:

- Assign a communications coordinator to the work plan, usually a member of Corporate Communications.
- Determination of the legal requirements for customer notification.
- Identify all groups who would receive project communication, including acquired bank employees.
- Identify types of communication appropriate for each group.
- Develop the format for communications (initial announcements, media, newsletter, letters, personal contacts, statement stuffers, etc.)
- Develop a schedule for communications.
- Issue the communications per schedule.
- Establish Q/A scripts for employees, managers.
- Develop administrative packages- travel information and guidelines, mail/communication information, expense claims.

Notification Plan

Approach

- The project will have a Communications Coordinator and Communication Team members who will work with the assigned Team members for each work plan. This is a critical project task and the individual selected for these tasks must have business line product exposure and excellent communication skills. The individuals must be available from the beginning of the conversion to the completion of the process. Depending on the types of customer impacts, and when they will occur, various mediums are used to communicate these to the customer:
  - Personal telephone calls or site visits
  - Letters
  - Statements Stuffers
  - Pamphlets describing changes
  - Q & A Scripts
  - Media

- The individuals will have the responsibility for determining what notification pieces are needed for the bank's customers; the initial drafts of the letters, working with Team Leaders to complete notifications on time, and keeping internal departments, customer service areas, and other defined individuals or departments abreast of all mailings.
- A review of all customer notifications by the Legal Department is also completed as part of this process.
- The Product/Pricing Team Leaders or Team Members within the Business Lines works closely with the Communications Team on this function. Information needed for customer notifications is largely obtained from product mapping and the resulting impacts analysis, along with any other new/changed information that will affect how a customer transacts business on their existing accounts.

Customer Communication Plan

This document is prepared and updated as necessary by the Communication Coordinator selected to coordinate the printing and mailing of all customer notifications. Maybe used jointly with the individual(s) assigned responsible for determining customer impacts.

Internal Notification Matrix

Development of an Internal Notification Matrix and procedures are critical to the success of this conversion. Internal departments must be notified of all customer communications prior to the customer contact. Procedures for responding to customer questions should be the responsibility of the Coordinator assigned to customer notification. The document should be updated regularly with current customer notification letters, and distributed to all related departments and various individuals. The document may also be distributed on the project team shared drive.

PHASE 2 DISCOVERY & ANALYSIS

Purpose

Deliverables

Product Line Disposition Document

Organization Definition document

Mapping questionnaire and product Mapping Sessions

Mapping Questionnaire Example

Product Mapping Document Example

Area Pricing Document

Data Base Mapping

Data Mapping Document

Account Re numbering Documentation

Account Renumbering Summary

General Ledger Account Documentation

General Ledger Translation Chart

Impact analysis sessions document

Impact Analysis Worksheet

Impact analysis Document

Customer impact document

Customer Impact/ Notification Document

Product Line Disposition Document

Responsibility	SYSTEMS COORDINATOR, assisted by SYSTEMS TEAM LEADERS
Description	For each product at the bank to be integrated, this document shows the current system on which It is processed, and the XXX application system(s) that this product will be processed on post integration. Information on all core and non-core systems from the due diligence phase should be reviewed prior to completing the Product Line Disposition Document.

Example:

PRODUCT LINE DISPOSITION DOCUMENT
(Example)

Completed by:
Contact Information:
Date:

PRODUCT	CURRENT XXX BANK SYSTEM	XXX SYSTEM

43

Organizational Definition Document

Responsibility   BUSINESS UNITS

Description   This document will outline the organization of the new organization as it will be in the XXX environment. This will include an outline of the number of branches/offices, districts, regions, etc. This information is required for G.L. hierarchy setup, central spoof setup, mapping, impact analysis, application, and department setup phases.

Mapping Questionnaire and Product Mapping Session and Documents

Responsibility   SYSTEMS and Operations TEAM LEADERS

Description   These sessions explore, discuss, and decide how to merge the new bank's products into the products supported through XXX. The objective is to complete the product mapping summary and comparison documents and at the same time identify customer, financial and operational impacts.

The bank(s) that will be merged will be asked to complete a thorough standard product information questionnaire for each product prior to the mapping sessions. The documents are organized to facilitate mapping to XXX standards. These will be used as the starting point in mapping products to the XXX system.

The individual(s) assigned the responsibility of completing this document should be extremely knowledgeable about these products. This same individual(s) must participate in the product mapping sessions. Product mapping sessions generally last 1 to 3 days for each application. (DDA, savings, etc.) How the product works, how it is priced, how it is supported (including any special handling), who the product's targeted audience is, product restrictions, and other related information will be discussed in detail.

These product mapping sessions are extremely critical to the overall success of the conversion process. The individuals

44

assigned to this task should come prepared to discuss this information in complete detail. In addition to product mapping documentation, impacts to customer, operations, budget, and staffing should be identified, and noted on Impact Documentation.

The information is used by product teams to determine possible changes to systems, impacts on customers or operations, and much of the detail needed for coding and setup of application.

Attendees   The potential list of attendees at these sessions may include product managers, systems, operations, individuals assigned to customer notification, and other individuals deemed necessary.

Approval   Representatives from both banks should review and approve finalized mapping documentation.

Example: (Example of Mapping Questionnaire and Product Mapping Document. These show examples of the types of product features that may be included for different products. This list is not complete. As each product is mapped, all features for each product should be discussed).

MAPPING QUESTIONNAIRE
(*Example*)

XXX Team Leader: **Contact Information:**
Response By: **Contact Information:**
XXX Product Name:
XXX Product Description:

Q #	Sample Features	Questions	Response
1.01	Processing System		
1.02			
2.01	System Identifiers		
2.02			
3.01	Volumes		
4.01	Limits		
5.01	Fees		
6.01	Calculation Methods		
7.01	Cutovers		

COUSINSGROUP

8.01	Balance Info		
9.01	Account # Format		
10.01	Reissue Team		
11.01	Account # Format		
12.01	Reissue/Renewal		
13.01	Late Charges		
14.01	Disclosure Agreement		
15.01	Statement Options		
16.01	Receipts		

PRODUCT MAPPING DOCUMENT
(*Example*)

XXX Team Leader: **Contact Information:**
XXX Product Name: **Bank XXX Product Name:**

Product Feature	XXX Product Name	Bank XX Product Name	Impact due to mapping to XXX standard	C N	F I	T R	P R	O T H	Pending Issue Y/N? #_____
Processing System									
System Identifiers									
Volumes									
Limits									
Fees									
Calculation Methods									
Cutovers									
Balance Info									
Account # format									

COUSINSGROUP

Reissue Team									
Account # Format									
Reissue/Renewal									
Late Charges									
Disclosure Agreement									
Statement Info Options									
Receipts									
G/L Inteface Req.									

CN   = Customer Notification
FI   = Financial Impact
TR   = Training Impact
PR   = Procedural Issue
OTH = Other Impact

Area Pricing Document

Responsibility   RETAIL COORDINATOR, RETAIL TASK FORCE

Description   Area pricing is the ability to set interest rates, many fees, and balance requirements at the market-sensitive levels. Branches are assigned to pre-determined market areas. While the application systems allow many area pricing options, it is the responsibility of the Retail Coordinator, in association with the Business Unit, to determine which pricing options will be available to area banks. It is recommended that area pricing options be determined prior to product mapping.

Each defined area must complete the appropriate area pricing setup document and forward to the Retail Coordinator at a specified time. The Retail Coordinator presents the completed area document to a central bank pricing committee for review. Once all issues are resolved, this document becomes the central piece for customer notification, disclosures, systems input, training and other

47

related areas. The Retail Coordinator will discuss the format of the Area Pricing Document with Team Leaders.

Pricing Options See the Retain Conversion Plan to determine all pricing options available under Area Pricing for:

- DDA
- SAVINGS
- OFFICIAL CHECKS
- CHECK CASHING/TRAVELERS CHECKS
- STATEMENT PRINT FEES
- MONEY ORDERS
- UTILITY FEES
- INSTALLMENT LOANS
- EQUITY LOANS
- CREDIT CARD
- OVERDRAFT PROTECTION
- SAFE DEPOSIT BOX

Database Mapping

Responsibility SYSTEMS and Operations TEAM LEADERS

Description Soon after product mapping is completed, and decisions finalized on where to map existing bank products to XXX, database mapping sessions are scheduled. The Data Mapping Document maps the individual data fields from the current system to the XXX Flat File, noting all the special features necessary for de-conversion programs. The information is used by programmers to write the de-conversion program, and sometimes used to setup the application. There is a data mapping document for each system. Each field is described in detail, and often takes the form of program specifications. Minutes of the database mapping meetings should be documented.

The bank(s) will be asked to complete or provide documentation that indicates all system fields that need to be compared to the XXX system.

Database mapping session generally last 1 to 2 days for each application (DDA, savings, etc.)

Issues and Impacts documents should be updated from results of the Data Mapping Sessions. Change Control Requests may also be generated from the results.

Attendees

The potential list of attendees at these sessions may include product management; individuals involved in product mapping, systems, operations, individuals assigned to customer notification, and other individuals deemed necessary.

Tools

<u>XXX System Documentation</u>
- File Layouts
- Field Definitions (Conversion Tables)
- Control Files
- Bank Options and Tables

<u>XXX User Documentation</u>
- Processing Procedures

<u>Converting Bank System Documentation</u>
- File Layouts
- Field Definitions (Conversion Tables)
- Control Files
- Bank Options and Tables

<u>Converting Bank User Documentation</u>
- Processing Procedures

<u>Completed Questionnaires</u>

<u>Product Mapping Documentation</u>

Signoff

After the Database Mapping Documents have been finalized, the documents should be reviewed from members of both banks. Concurrence of how data fields have been mapped should be documented, including names, titles, and signatures.

Mapping Format

<u>Heading</u>
- Document Name
- Project Name

- XXX System Name
- Submitted By

Mapping Scope

This should include brief overview of which accounts will be converted. It should include a statement of whether closed accounts will be converted within specified dates. It will also include a statement of which accounts will not be converted (i.e. charge offs, inactive), or which accounts will be converted to a different system.

Mapping Specifications

For each XXX flat file field, a statement should be made as to how the field show be filled using the converting bank data (converting bank field names). It may include "IF" and "Else" statements, calculation data, or specify converting bank codes used to set the XXX field value.

Example:

Product Mapping Document
XXXX INTEGRATION PROJECT

Product Feature	CMA Prod Name	Bank XX Prod name	Impact Due to mapping to CMA	CN	FI	TR	PR	OTH	Pend issu Y/N

CN= Customer Notification

FI= Financial Impact

TR= Training Impact

PR= Procedural Issue

OTH=Other Impact

Account Renumbering Documentation

Responsibility	SYSTEMS TEAM LEADERS or ACCOUNT NUMBERING TEAM LEADER
Distribution	Systems Coordinator (or Account Renumbering Coordinator), Impacted Coordinators/Team Leaders, Communications Coordinator or Team Members
Description	This documentation records all relevant information about account numbers currently used in all systems at the consolidated bank, as well as all number that will be supported after conversion.

Decisions will be made with regard to renumbering, check reissue, card reissue, coupon reissue, cross reference files, routing and transit number changes, ACH/Wire effects, PIN changes, telephone banking, servicing changes, and reissue of printed customer documents.

The assigned coordinator and team will develop solutions, and ensure that processing and customer impacts are addressed.

Purpose	The information is used to setup MICR editing, and application systems. It is also used to identify issues with account numbering early in the integration process, and then to document the decisions made on these issues.
Chart	An account number reference chart for each account number type is created noting:

- Account Type
- T/R
- Digits
- Format
- Check Digit Routine
- Range specific information
- Process Control Codes (to select check digit routines)
- Numbers used
- CIF Information

A decision is then made with regard to the need for account renumbering and the method of renumbering.

Account Renumbering Summary Document

51

An Account Renumbering Summary Document must be created and distributed to appropriate parties nothing the following information:

- Application
- Note Application Name

Renumber Volume

Calculate population of accounts requiring renumbering. Specify accounts. Indicate if accounts will be renumbered prior to, or at core conversion and scheduled distribution time.

Renumber Reason

- Account length
- Duplicates
- Format to standard

Processing Impact

- Routing/Transit updates
- New Checks order and distribution
- ACH effects/Wire effects
- Telephone banking effects
- Coupon changes
- Card reissue
- PIN changes
- Cross Reference Tables required
- Service Inquiry Changes
- Internal Document changes (if not destroyed)
- Other preprinted customer documents

Customer Impact/Date Required

- Coupon Book Reissue
- Check Reissue
- Card Reissue
- Notification Only
- Routing/Transit instruction changes

Example:

ACCOUNT RENUMBERING SUMMARY
XXXX INTEGRATION PROJECT
(*Example*)

Submitted by: **Contact Information:**

Application	Renumber Volume	Renumber Reason	Processing Impacts	Customer Impacts

General Ledger Account Documentation

Responsibility	SYSTEMS ANALYST (TEAM MEMBERS), OPERATIONS ANALYSTS (TEAM MEMBERS)
Distribution	Systems Coordinator, Operations Coordinator, Impacted Coordinators/Team Leaders, Communications Coordinator or Team Member
Description	The general ledger, A/P, Fixed Asset, and Payroll conversions generally precede the Application conversions. In the period after general ledger conversion, but prior to application conversion, accounts used by systems and operations need to be identified and translated to the XXX general ledger. Daily file transmission of the translated data occurs. This documentation provides the basis for the translation of their GL account and Cost Center numbers to corresponding XXX Accounts and cost centers.
Purpose	The information is published to other Teams and used in application setup, impact analysis, training, department setup (forms requirements, procedure writing, etc.)
Method	For each operations and system area, the account number and cost center numbers used by each group will be identified concurrently with the impact analysis. From this information, the General Ledger Accounts Translation Chart will be constructed.

Example:

GENERAL LEDGER TRANSLATION CHART
XXXX INTEGRATION PROJECT
(*Example*)

Submitted By: **Contact Information:**
Team: **Date:**

Account Name	XXX GL Account	XXX Cost Center	Bank XX GL Account(s)	Bank XX Cost Center(s)
DDA Personal	1234567	All	7777777	1111 2222 3333 4444

54

Impact Analysis Sessions and Document

Responsibility   TEAM LEADERS

Distribution   Team members, Group Coordinators, Impacted Coordinators/Team Leaders, Communications Coordinator or Team Members.

Description   Impact analysis is used to identify how the converting bank environment will change as a result of conversion to XXX standard operating policies and procedures.

The final deliverables for this task is an Impacts Document which identifies both internal and customer impacts which will occur as a result of a conversion/consolidation to the XXX standard operating policies, procedures, etc., by acquiring member bank must be taken into consideration). Each function should by analyzed to determine impacts to processing methods, timeframes, system access, departmental controls, work flow, forms, reports, screens, equipment, etc.

It is not necessary to document the processes in the bank to be integrated. Only differences between the converting bank from XXX standards should be noted. It is very important to insure that all functions are analyzed; therefore it is very important to understand all specialized handling that is required for any customer, group, or officer. It maybe advisable to determine top customers and any related special processing to ensure impact is minimized. The Impact Document is comprised of the following elements (see example on page____)

Purpose

The information contained on the Impact Analysis is used as a basis for many of the remaining integration tasks. Differences and impacts identified are used to:

- Define manner of handling all impacts.
- Tailor necessary training.
- Ensure staffing, organization, and equipment is properly set-up.
- Identify tasks needed for organizational readiness.
- Identify new forms of procedures needed.
- Identify internal and external required communications.

Tools

Required Information

The following information is required to begin the process of Impact Identification:

- Operations, business, and systems personnel familiar with the new and old environments
- Review of existing Assumptions/Decisions.
- Review of Product Mapping Documentation.
- New organizational definition document.
- Current XXX Process Documentation.
- Converting Bank Procedural Documentation.
- Lists and examples of forms (both environments).
- List and examples of reports (both environments).
- List and examples of screens (both environments).
- Copies of training information for standard functions.
- Questionnaires for each work plan to be completed by the converting bank prior to interview sessions.
- Interview fact sheets for each function.
- Impact Analysis Document.

Impact Form

Impact Number

Assign a number to each impact statement. Only include functions where the Integrated bank functions differently from the XXX standard.

Function

- Indicate the name of the bank being analyzed when a converting bank is compromised of more than one community bank.
- Indicate the name of the workstation/function being analyzed; e.g., file clerk, accounting clerk, documentation preparation.
- Indicate the name of the individual(s) interviewed as a representative for a particular workstation/function.
- List the operational attributes analyzed for possible operational and/or customer impacts within an individual workstation/function.
- An operational function maybe comprised of one workstation/person or a number of workstations/people completing the same task.

XXX Standard

Describe the XXX standard for this function.

Impacts and Resolutions

- List the impacts/differences between the converting bank and XXX bank environments as determined during the workstation interview process.
- As resolutions to impacts are decided, document the manner in which the impact will be handled.

Assign/Date

Indicate the individual(s) responsible for obtaining a resolve to each impact/difference listed in the Impacts Document. List the required resolution date.

Impact

Indicate the areas affected by the change in process or environment:

- Staff
- Procedure
- Form
- Report
- Training

- Equipment

Issue Y/N

Indicate if the impact will become an open issue that requires a resolution, and therefore needs to be added to the Issues/Assumptions/Decisions List.

Cross Impact Areas

Indicate all other areas that will be impacted by changes. Distribute the highlighted document to the other areas indicated. Note Communications and Training groups, as applicable.

Miscellaneous   Customer Impacts

All impacts affecting customers should be detailed on the Customer Impact Document (See page 58). The Customer Impact Document is used to coordinate and develop Customer Notification Strategies.

Impacts Review Meeting

An Impacts Review Meeting is held after the interview process for each function/workstation and the initial draft of the Impacts Document has been completed. The meeting will provide an opportunity to:

- Review/verify the impacts/differences outlined in the Impacts Document. Decide if the impact is ongoing. Resolve issues, or update issues list.
- Assign the open items to the appropriate individuals for a resolution within assigned time frames. Where necessary, Change Control Requests maybe completed. Decide if some issues will be assigned as conversion clean-up tasks.
- Representatives from both banks and the Communications Team should attend the review meetings. Internal communications may need to be developed as a result of impact analysis.
- Review impacts with training and incorporate changes into training materials.

Impact Analysis Worksheet

The following information maybe used to identify impacts, but is not intended to be a complete list of all categories of impacts:

Organizational

- Are there any job role changes?
- Are there to be FTE changes?
- Are there interdepartmental changes?
- Are there organizational changes that will affect other departments?
- Do Management changes affect this department?
- Are mechanisms in place to communicate changes made in your area or other areas?

Procedural

- Are there department function changes?
- Will information, data, and reports be coming from a different place? Time? Format? Number of copies? Distribution mode?
- What are the policy differences?
- What are the control differences: Dollar limits, volume limits, authorization levels, signature cards, oral verifications, balancing controls, personal authority levels, quality controls?
- Is there a change in how the information will come to the user?
- Does it require a different report, screen, form? What local logs, forms, checklists, files are used? Are reports created manually on a PC?
- What customer agreements, contractual obligations, or legal agreements are used? What information is sent outside the bank (i.e. SBA, agencies, etc.)
- What information does customer receive? Format?
- Contact Lists? Other departmental contact? Help functions?
- Even if a form is the same, will it change due to new account numbers? Tran codes, etc.?
- How will forms be processed? Ordered?
- Will account, officers, branch, district/region, GL numbers change?
- Will other codes change?
- How will procedures change?
- Will training or retraining be required? How?
- How will product changes be communicated? Does this change procedure?
- What special handling requirements are required for specified customers? Officers? Departments?
- Are there system access changes? What access is required?
- Is a function being eliminated or added to an area? FTE impact?

- Will there be changes in the amount of time needed to perform a task? FTE impact? Are there changes in volume?
- Are equipment changes needed?
- Are there differences in departmental controls?
- Will some forms be retained? Destroyed?
- What screens are used? Is any information on screens not available in the new environment?
- Are there any automated or manual system changes?
- Are there any management or tracking changes?
- Do other departments need to change as a result of changes in this department?
- Will changes be phased in or implemented suddenly?
- How will you assure that our procedures will be adhered to by other departments?
- Are there responsibility changes that you need to coordinate with other departments?

Cultural

- Are there any changes that will affect employee morale?
- Will the organization be able to adopt the new procedures, changes, etc.?
- Does the department support the changes?
- How will changes affect customers? Directors? Shareholders?
- How will changes be communicated to other departments?
- What expectations do others have of your department? Will these change?

Customer

- Will the changes in your department be seamless to customers?
- How should changes be communicated to customers?
- Will the customer be receptive to changes?
- What negative customer affects will there be?

Schedule/Size

- Are there proper resources in place to execute changes?
- What tasks/activities in your area are on the project critical path?
- Are you dependent on others to complete activities?

Example:

IMPACT ANALYSIS DOCUMENT
(*Example*)

Project Name:
Work Plan Name:
Team Leader:
Contact Information:

| # | Function | XXX Standard | Impact and Resolution | Assigned To/Date | IMPACT | | | | | | Issue Y/N | Cross Impact Areas |
					Staff	Proc	Form	Rept	Train	Equip		
Ex. 1	Credit Admin: Collection Policy Past Due Reporting is biweekly. Officer begins collections at 15 days.	XXX Officers begin collection at 10 days. Past due report is weekly.	TR: Provide training on new report, policy. Officer: Follow new collection policy.	TR: J. Smith					X		N	Ln. Rev.

Customer Impact Document

Responsibility	TEAM LEADERS/COMMUNICATION TEAM MEMBERS
Distribution	Team Members, Group Coordinators, Impacted Coordinators/Team leaders, Communications Coordinator or Team Member
Description	The Customer Impact Analysis Document is used to summarize how all changes will impact customers and the approach to notifying customers as necessary. This analysis is used as a source for development of the customer notification strategies. It is used to ensure that the notifications are complete and coordinated. The Customer Impact Document is comprised of the following elements (see example on Page ____)

COUSINSGROUP

Tools   Required Information
                       The Customer Impact Document is developed from information
                       gathered during Work flow Analysis. Information is then
                       summarized on the Customer Impact Analysis document.

Customer Impact Form

               Product
               Name of product with Customer Impact

               Description of Customer Impact
               Briefly describe the customer impact.

               Method of communication
               Indicate the method(s) of communication to the customer.

               Customer Group
               Will all customers using that product be affected, or only a portion?
               Indicate which customer segment would be affected.

               Number of Customers
               Determine the number of customers that need to be notified.

               Date of Communication
               Determine the required date of the communication, noting legal
               requirement dates.

Results   Use of Form
                       Information from the customer Impact Analysis Document will be
                       included in the Communication Plan, and serve as an outline for the
                       contents of the related communications.

Example:

CUSTOMER IMPACT/NOTIFICATION DOCUMENT
(*Example*)

Project Name:
Work Plan Name:
Team Leader   **Communication Team Member:**
Contact Information: **Contact Information:**

Product	Description of Customer Impact	Method of Communication	Customer Group	No. of Customers	Date of Communication

PHASE 3 READINESS

Phase Objective

The Readiness Phase of the project will plan, supervise, and coordinate all department activities necessary for the conversion of all affiliates to the products and procedures of the newly created XXX bank.

Deliverables

Department Set- up

Department Set-up Checklist

Training Delivery

Survival Guides

Organizational Readiness Meetings

Critical success factors List

Application Set-up

Coding, Unit and System Testing

Unit/system Test Scope Document

Integrated Testing/ Validation Testing: Test Controls

Integrated Test Scope Document

Production/Capacity Testing

Production/Volume Test Scope Document

Test Scripts/Test transactions

Test Plans/Test Calendar

Unit and integrated Test Communication Plan

Department Setup

Responsibility   ASSIGNED TEAM LEADERS

Description   Organizational Readiness Meetings will begin to transfer ownership and responsibility for this project from the project team to the converted bank.

The meetings will answer the questions:
1. Are you prepared for this conversion?
2. Are you prepared to perform your job when this conversion is completed?
3. Are you prepared to service the customer?
4. What are the tasks you must have completed prior to the merger to be ready for the new environment?
5. How are the operating units, as opposed to the project team, taking ownership for execution of tasks?
6. What are your critical success factors?

Responsibilities <u>Team Leaders</u>

- Perform workflow impact analysis to determine differences in operation procedures, forms, supplies needed, etc. Document changes to current environment.
- Determine department setup requirements, including Organizational Structure, Training Schedules and delivery, Staffing, Procedure development and distribution, forms, equipment ordering and installation, supplies, office ownership assignments, employee logon IDs and related security issues (IDs, network security testing, etc.)
- Formulate and manage implementation plan for all of the above requirements.
- Determine report needs and distribution requirements.
- Determine customer service needs and develop a plan for providing all of the necessary support functions to assist in minimizing customer impacts, both during the conversion and after.

<u>Tools</u>

- Manuals of standard forms, by area.

- List of standard reports, by area.
- Security setup forms.
- Express setup forms.
- Impact Analysis and fact sheets, including identification of procedural changes.
- Customer Impact Analysis List.
- Training Schedules.
- Procedure Manuals, by function.
- Current Service Level Agreements.

Typical Setup Tasks

- Determine and staff departments. Resolve HR issues.
- Determine training needs. Develop and deliver Training. Develop supplemental "Survivor Guides".
- Determine customer service impacts, and ensure processes and notifications are in place to address each (in coordination with Communication Team)
- Determine and inform external parties- i.e. vendors, armored carriers, etc.
- Determine and complete database cleanup requirements- duplicates, deletions, additions.
- Participate in cross impacts analysis.
- Determine, order, and install equipment. Dispose of equipment not needed.
- Determine, plan, execute physical plant changes.
- Determine, setup, and test security access.
- Setup Central Proof (hierarchy) - Retail/Ops
- Determine, order, deliver forms & stationary. Destroy old forms.
- Determine deadlines. Determine impact of missing them, and how to recover.
- Determine, modify, and distribute procedures (coordinate with training). Develop new procedures according to XXX standards, as needed.
- Resolve outstanding issues.
- Determine reports distribution requirements and endpoints. Deliver worksheets.
- Determine (modify) and distribute Service Level Agreements.
- Complete central proof setup.

- Complete network testing.
- Complete Organizational Readiness Checklist for Organizational Readiness Meetings.
- Determine Critical Success Factors.
- Obtain appropriate signoffs.

Example:

DEPARTMENT SETUP CHECKLIST
(Example)

Work Plan:
Team Leader:
Contact Information:

#	FUNCTION	ASSIGNED RESOURCE	DUE DATE	STATUS	COMMENTS
1.0	Staffing				
1.1					
1.2					
2.0	Deadlines				
3.0	Procedures				
4.0	Security				
5.0	Forms				
6.0	Equipment				
7.0	Physical Layout				
8.0	Training/Survival Guides				
9.0	Customer Service				
10.0	Reports				
11.0	Network Test (Retail/Ops only)				
12.0	Central Proof Setup (Retail only)				

Training Delivery

Responsibility   TRAINING COORDINATOR, TEAM LEADERS

Approach   A Training Coordinator will be assigned to act as a liaison between the Corporate Training department, the individual systems, operations, and business line teams and the management at the converting bank. The Training Coordinator, working with members

67

COUSINSGROUP

of the bank Work Plan Teams, will plan, develop, schedule, and deliver training materials.

Description   General Philosophy
- Training plans will be "audience" driven.
- Employees will be trained on "changes".
- Training will be developed/delivered using a multi-media approach, including the following methods:
  - Paper-based
  - Classroom "hands-on"
  - Video
  - Computer Based Training (CBT)
  - Computer Based Reference (CBR)
  - Informal training
  - Quick Reference tools
  - Self-Instructional Module
- XXX "standards" will be used for each delivery method.
- Development/delivery of training will use Adult Learning Theories such as:
  - "How" things are being changed.
  - Logical sequence.
  - Provided in visual medium.
  - Enhancement through "hands-on".
  - Relate to, or understanding "why".
- Training process must include the "encouragement" of and the "demonstration" of how to use reference material in the future environment (i.e. Computer Based Reference=CBR)
- Assurance of consistency and quality within all aspects of training.
- User management is responsible for ensuring employees are trained.

Strategy
- Curriculum is developed on specific needs.
- Delivery is via "functional" training vs. "application".
- Curriculum is built around changes to existing environment in the bank(s) being acquired.
- Ensure multi-media techniques are applied to curriculum plans for each audience.

- Utilize development and delivery standards that have been incorporated into previous conversion efforts.
- Deliver classroom training through a "facilitator" vs. "instructor led" technique.
- Provide employees with the opportunity to practice; simulate "real life" situations in which to apply learning.
- Provide "hand-on" experience using reference materials.
- Make training systems available to practice/refresh learning as needed.

Additional Support Techniques

- Train in "stages" such that most critical pieces of training are closest to conversion date and each piece reinforces the previous.
- Provide opportunity to take CBTs in a lab or designated workstation environment.
- Material reviewed by appropriate individuals (i.e. subject matter experts) for content, consistency, quality, accuracy, and to ensure needs of users will be met.
- Conduct pilot training sessions to provide opportunity for evaluation prior to full rollout of training sessions.
- Conduct management orientation sessions to obtain support and inform of specific roles/responsibilities of all involved.

- Retail may conduct a Training Expo to provide overview of training materials, "hands-on" classroom simulation, etc., prior to actual start of training sessions to begin familiarizing employees with terms, equipment, etc.

- Conduct follow-up evaluations of all sessions to make improvements to training and to provide additional support/training to employees as needed.

- Reinforce/Evaluate comprehension of information on which employees are trained (for example, this could be done through a fun, quiz-type game).

69

Responsibilities

Training Coordinator and Team

- Coordinates all training activities for the conversion effort; works with system, operations, and line work team members to ensure adherence to XXX conversion training philosophies and strategies.
- Promotes XXX training philosophies.
- Facilitates curriculum quality review, publishing, facilitator training, site, equipment, setup, scheduling, approvals, and adherence to work plans. Coordination of Expos.
- Coordinates informal training.
- Coordinates executive training.
- Distributes Master Training Schedules.

Training Team Leader (each Work Team)

- Develops the detailed work plan for ensuring the development and delivery of all necessary "change" information to employees.
- Identifies audiences and facility/equipment needs to cover these audiences.
- Reviews product changes and impact analysis documents to obtain foundations for training curriculum needed; also uses these documents to determine issues and assumptions.
- Develops curriculum plans, identifying subject matter, and obtaining sign-off from the appropriate user management.
- Assists in identifying bank employees to serve as training facilitators for the conversion effort, ensures their preparation/education and oversees the detailed curriculum development by this training team.
- Develops and coordinates the training schedules for all employees identified to receive training.
- Leads the preparation of delivery of classroom pilots for all courses to be offered; evaluates and makes appropriate changes as required to curriculum before formal delivery of courses.
- Assists in the delivery of courses.
- Evaluates success of classroom sessions, both from trainer and participants evaluations.

- Coordinates/Oversees "student" progress reporting to user management to ensure employees receive any additional training/support as needed (reporting is provided by Corporate Training and Development)
- Assists with analysis to ensure adherence to critical success factors of the project.
- Participates in post training support activities such as Help line, Problem Log review, and site visits.

Key Training Activities

Curriculum Development

- With the aid of XXX Training and Development and the Training Coordinator, the Training Team Leaders and the selected trainers develop the needed curriculum, providing customization as required to the standard product and process curriculum that has been developed for conversion training.
- The impact analysis documents serve to provide the basis for identifying "changes" requiring training.

Quality Review

- The objective of the quality review is to reconfirm training decisions and finalize the training plan. The review takes place approximately 60 days prior to conversion. Participants in the quality review may include:
  - Line Management
  - Subject Matter experts
  - Auditors
  - Product Management
  - Appropriate Conversion Team members

Scheduling

- The Training Team Leaders coordinates the scheduling of all employees for the appropriate session(s), taking into consideration each employee's job description when enrolling them for the various courses.
- Business lines should be involved in the scheduling process to ensure adequate staff coverage throughout the training process.

- Every effort should be made to train employees as close to the conversion date(s) as possible to ensure that information learned can be applied within 30 days whenever possible.
- Classroom sessions consist of 8-12 employees per session.

Product

- The Product/Pricing Team Leader oversees this aspect of training, covering all changes to existing products and their accompanying policies, fees, etc.
- Generally, this training can occur in larger group sessions as there is no "hands-on" application.
- A complete product guide should be produced to assist employees in learning detailed information about the new products.
- This training should occur prior to the mailing of customer notification booklets.

Survival Guides

Responsibility   TEAM LEADERS (only Retail has delivered these in the past, but other areas may incorporate them).

Description   Survival Guides are prepared by the Team Leaders to assist employees in making the transition at each phase of converting to XXX systems, procedures, etc.

Survival Guides are prepared to supplement training that has been provided, outline any "last minute" changes in procedures/forms/products (as required), provide resource information, and phone numbers.

Survival Guides provide detailed instructions for "walking through" transitional activities.

Checklists of forms and supplies needed are provided to ensure implementation of appropriate paperwork, etc.

"Last day" activities are also detailed.

72

Organizational Readiness Meetings

Responsibility   IPO MANAGER, COORDINATORS

Description   Organizational Readiness meetings are generally held during the last two or four months prior to conversion; these meeting replace the monthly IPO Manager's meetings that have been taking place throughout the project, and may occur on a more frequent basis (weekly); the Integration Leader and IPO Manager will determine at what point these meetings should begin.

        On the basis of these meetings, a "go" decision will be made. The meetings begin to transfer ownership of the integration from the project team to the acquired bank.

        Meetings should review Organizational Readiness Checklists developed during Department Setup in the Readiness Phase.

        Attendees at these meetings are the IPO Manager, Project Coordinators, various Team Leaders and Work Plan Staff, business management and users, representatives from the bank affiliate(s) being acquired, and others as required.

        The purpose of these meetings is to coordinate final plans for the conversion, resolving any remaining issues and ensuring that all areas know their responsibilities in detail from this point through the weekend in order to get all systems, procedures, products, etc., fully implemented to XXX.

        All participants should be able to state that their respective area has completed all necessary tasks, (testing, setup, etc.) needed to implement a successful conversion, and is in complete readiness to provide customers with uninterrupted service.

        Participants should also develop Critical Success Factors on which to measure the effectiveness of the implementation.

Critical Success Factors List

Responsibility   TEAM LEADERS, working with PRODUCTION AND BUSINESS LINE MANAGERS NESSARY

Description   Working with production or business line management, a list of Critical Success Factors will detail the elements identified as critical to conduct "business as usual" immediately following the conversion.

Each project team's responsiveness to these factors will determine the level of success of the conversion.

As the factors are identified, the Team Leader will verify that all necessary tasks have been accomplished to ensure that critical success factors are met.

The Team Leader and the Business Line or Production Manager will also identify what should be done if an unavoidable problem is encountered. One critical success factor will be how quickly and effectively problems are corrected.

If a critical success factor is dependent on another area or system, it will be the Team Leader's responsibility to verify required tasks have been performed.

Critical success factors should be specific: i.e. all DDA overdraft reports will be delivered by _____ AM.

The Team Leader will incorporate review of the Critical Success Factors into the Post Support Implementation Check List.

Application Setup

Responsibility   SYSTEMS AND OPERATIONS TEAM LEADERS

Description   Application setup will plan and create processing schedules.

Steps   Determine Conversion File Requirements
                        • Determine the amount of file space that will be required for test and conversion files.

74

- Complete a "disk space request" form and submit it to the DASD Coordinator.

Determine Production File Requirements

- Determine the amount of new file space required for production files after conversion.
- Complete "disk space request" memo and submit it to the DASD Coordinator.

Document File Retention

- Determine and document file retention periods and location for all test and conversion files. (Production files will have the same retention as normal production files.)

Create Processing Files

- Establish all production data sets by running the file create utility, and all files required for this application.

Create Production Job Status

- Set up JCL job streams for all production jobs according to the required standards.

Create Production Control Documentation/Turnover to Production Control

- Develop all documentation required for Production Control according to the Data Processing Standards manual. The documentation and JCL from each team must be turned over to the Production Control Department at least 6 weeks prior to processing.

Develop Unit Test Plan

- Develop a system test plan, including individual programs and job streams.

Setup Test Files and Test JCL

- Establish all test data sets.

Determine Processing Schedules

- Review all processing schedules currently in effect at the stie. Determine critical "processing windows" that must remain, and

COUSINSGROUP   All rights reserved 2001-2012

where schedules could be altered. Establish agreed upon time frames.

- Obtain signoff from the users on new schedules.

Coding, Unit, and System Testing

Responsibility   TEST COORDINATOR, SYSTEMS TEAMS ANALYSTS

Description   Flat File

- "Flat Files" were designed with the intention of simplifying the process by which Data Mapping and Conversion Programming is done. The file conversion is divided into two sections:

  1. The "conversion" programs which convert the new bank's files to a standard or "flat file"
  2. The "load" programs which convert the flat file into the production format. A very detailed Data Dictionary should be developed for each flat. The result is:
     - The programming staff at either bank could write the conversion programs.
     - Service bureaus could write the programs.
     - Programmers do not have to be application experts.
     - Programming and unit testing of the conversion programs can be done independently.
     - Prior conversion programs can be used as models.
     - Some data mapping can begin before product mapping is completed.

Unit and System Testing

In order to complete Unit Testing, participants should have a thorough knowledge of what types of input should produce what output from the system. Participants should also have knowledge of accounts and transactions having the right test features. The users from the converting bank participate in this review. Unit Testing will follow these steps:

- Develop Test Criteria- Create a document defining the requirements for all test data that will be required for both unit

76

and integrated testing. This will include transaction types and volumes of transactions to complete a thorough test of the system.

- Identify or create accounts/transactions for each item test.
- Create Test Files/Unit Test Conversion Programs.
- Verify "Last Day" processing, include accruals.
- Validate Conversion Programming Logic.
- Test Flat File load programs.
- Test Balancing procedures.
- Verify converted product and bank control data.
- Execute Batch Posting Testing.
- Review all output/verify results.
- Correct Problems, as necessary.
- Deliverables (Informal – within Teams)
  - Scope
  - Test Plan/Master Test Plan
  - Test Communication Plan
  - Chronological Calendar
  - Problem Form
  - Status Reporting

Example:

Unit Unit/System Test Scope Document

Project Name:
Test Coordinator:
Date Scheduled: **mm/dd/yy – mm/dd/yy (__ weeks)**
Date of file to be used: **mm/dd/yy (Iteration #)**
                                    mm/dd/yy (Iteration #)
                                    mm/dd/yy (Iteration #)

Project Objective:
Find and correct any mapping or coding errors in the conversion and/or merge of data from XXX systems to the XXX System.

Specific Responsibilities:
- Capture master files from the servers and from bank being merged into. (All)
- Create extracts for cross referencing old account numbers and create a cross reference file.
- Convert core applications on receipt of shells and/or merge and balance to GL.

77

- Pass files to UBS after integration and again after merge. (DDA,etc)
- Reconcile applications to GL
- Prepare Integrity Test.
- Verify Cross reference of account numbers is functioning properly. (All)
- Verify Account linkage. (CIF, CORE)
- Verify flat file data elements to database/product mapping. (All)
- Verify front-end bank/application edits and controls. (All)
- Verify merge process has successfully merged accounts as branches. (All – Merges only)
- Verify and take appropriate action to correct duplicates from the merge.
- Verify converted data to XXX systems. (All)
- Review output with customers (users) via the online and obtain approval.

Does not include:

- Online transaction entry will be part of Integrated Testing.
- Continued batch processing or daily posting will be part of Integrated Testing.
- Vendor last day processing will be tested during Validation Testing.
- List applications not participating and reasons.

Integrated Testing/Validation Testing: Test Controls

Responsibility   TEST COORDINATOR, SYSTEMS/Operations TEAM LEADERS

Test Coordinator Role

A test coordinator will be appointed by the Project Director to coordinate the integrated/validation testing, and will perform the following functions:
- Establishes a high level test scope and schedule.
- Consolidates detailed integrated test plans from all teams into a single master detailed plan.
- Prepares the Team Leader matrix.
- Establishes an integrated test log and problem reporting process.
- Establishes a status reporting process.
- Insures log ID's for Broadcast messages regarding test activity, problems, status reporting, and reminders.

- Schedules and runs team meetings with all teams participating in integrated testing.
- Sets up and modifies DASD test space, as required.
- Sets up priority with production control for test times.
- Ensures appropriate plans and assignments for validation of test results.

Integrated Testing

Integrated testing will test relationships between systems, using the following criteria:

- Use of moderate transaction volume.
- Feeds in test data transactions (MICR, on-line, electronic, etc.)
- Involves transaction input, and Day 0, 1 and 2 output verification. Day 2 is run as month end processing.
- Simulates production in a controlled environment.
- Confirm all system interaction within and between applications.
- Test Express (report distribution) endpoint destinations.
- Full testing of approved change control items.
- Validate control and balancing procedures.

Example:

Unit/System Test Scope Document
(*Example*)

Project Name:
Test Coordinator:
Date Scheduled: mm/dd/yy – mm/dd/yy (__ weeks)
Date of file to be used: mm/dd/yy (Iteration #)
                 mm/dd/yy (Iteration #)
                 mm/dd/yy (Iteration #)

Project Objective:
Using moderate transaction volume, simulate production in a controlled environment, confirming all system interaction within an application and to other applications, while verifying control and balancing procedures are correct.

Specific Responsibilities:
- Setup test files and JCL to be used during Integrated Testing.
- Test Express endpoint distribution, including Optical Disk, etc. and.
- Test daily processing after conversion using mm/dd as the processing date.

- Test month end processing using mm/dd as the processing date.
- Reformat files from ACH, XXX.
- Convert mm/dd/yy files, balance, and verify bank.
- Enter online transactions for the following applications.
- Pass interface files to verify continued processing for the following areas:
- Verify cross reference files.
- Verify the results with the users and obtain approval.

Does not include:
- Photocopy retrieval will be side tested.
- MICR transaction forms will be coordinated by IP.
- Reruns will be done as side-testing is necessary and will not be specifically planned for.
- Test of logons and System Access for branches will be done in the Network test.
- Test of logons, System Access will be done from mm/dd to mm/dd using Production Test Files, and be conducted by the Operations Team Leader with Production Control responsible for bringing for bringing up the online.
- Volume, PC job scheduling, PC deadlines, and production JCL will be tested in the Production Test.
- Last day processing, file cleanup with the most current files, and application processing will be verified in the Validation Test.
- Other applications not included (or tested later) and reason.

Production (Capacity) Testing

Responsibility   TEST COORDINATOR, SYSTEM TEAM LEADERS

Description   Production (Capacity) Testing

- Used to verify that capacity is adequate regarding hardware and deadlines.
- Use of full transaction volume from recent new bank files.
- Conduct 1st shift test for 5 days to cleanup JCL errors.
- Production control conducts 3rd shift test and provides incident reports for distribution.
- Conversion Call Matrix is developed.
- Requires substantial manipulations of file data in order to run the new bank production data in converted programs.
- Validates all application setup, including JCL.
- Verify deadlines in Production Control and for couriers.

- Deliverables:
  - Scope
  - Test Plan
  - Incidents Reports
  - Production Call matrix
  - Status reporting

Example:

Unit/System Test Scope Document

Project Name:
Test Coordinator:
Date Scheduled: mm/dd/yy – mm/dd/yy (__ weeks)
Date of file to be used: mm/dd/yy (CIF, ATM,)
                           mm/dd/yy (Masters and transactions)

Project Objective:
Verify applications setups (including JCL and Production Control Scheduling), courier deadlines, and hardware capacity, using FULL transaction volume.

Specific Responsibilities:
- Develop a call matrix to be used by Production Control (PC) for any problems found.
- Insure that production JCL, files, and DASD allocations are setup correctly.
- Insure that remote printing functions properly and is distributed correctly.
- Exception test Express Delivery, including Optical Disk.
- Balance input transactions to output and verify that output reports are on the correct media and distributed properly.
- Verify that (remote printing) transmission times/capacities are adequate.

81

- Bring any deficiencies found in handling third shift processing relative to the objectives to the attention of Technical Services, and Performance and Capacity Reporting.
- Execute the jobs in a production environment identifying problems.
- Verify that the processing meets required deadlines and does not adversely impact the other application deadlines.
- Recommend alternatives to correct any deficiencies found in handling third shift processing relative to the objectives.
- The following applications will be included in the third shift batch processing: (INSERT SYSTEMS)
- (Application examples)/ATM applications will contain minimum data requirements for batch processing, such as a date header.

Does not include:

- Online entry will not be part of the test. Access will be verified during the Security/Access Test, which is separate from this test.
- Non-daily processing (weekly, quarterly, yearly on request) will not be part of this test.

Test Scripts/Test Transactions

Responsibility　　　　SYSTEM TEAMS, Operations TEAMS as needed

Description　　　　　Test scripts will identify all account types and transaction types for which testing is required within the Testing Phase.

Specific test transaction accounts should be identified and transactions will be created via MICR documents, online entry, and electronic files.

Each application will identify the expected results (field entries or other output) that will be used to verify appropriate processing of the various types of transactions handled by each application.

Within the integrated testing, results will be verified. If results are not as expected, additional programming changes, problems reports, or change controls could result.

Test Scripts should identify the parties responsible for validating the results of the testing.

Testing control criteria must be detailed (i.e., financial accounts, record counts) and tested during this process.

Examples of Test Transactions:

The types of transactions will differ by application, so the below list is only a sample of transaction types. For each transaction type, appropriate verification fields would be identified. Attention would be given to testing available tran codes for specific account types. Tests may involve multiple day processing.

Example:

Test Plans/Test Calendar (combined format)

Responsibility   SYSTEMS TEAMS (Systems Analyst), IMPLEMENTATION COORDINATOR

Description   Detailed project plans cover high level test tasks. Each application will also generate detailed test plans, indicating system test requirements, and dependencies.

The Teams will deliver these requirements to the Test Coordinator.

The Test Coordinator will add start and end dates (Day 0, 1, and 2), and generate a master test schedule.

Test Plans should be published both by Test Start Date and by staff resource assigned.

Task ID #	Task Name	Task Notes	Resource	Dur.	Start	End	Predecessors	Status

83

Unit and Integrated Test Communication Plan

Responsibility   INTEGRATED TEST COORDINATOR

Description   The Test Communication Plans would be prepared in memo format and should state the following information:

- Status Reporting Schedule (Teams and Coordinator. (time of day)
- Method for participants to report daily status.
- Method that Coordinator will use to broadcast general status to all team leaders and interested parties. (Distribution List)
- Setup/test requirements for access to shared files.
- Method of preparing problem reports.
- Broadcast requirements of problems/delays.

Problem Form/Incident Reports

Responsibility   SYSTEM TEAM LEADERS, PRODUCTION CONTROL,

Process established by TEST COORDINATOR

Description   The problem form is used to report or update problems within the unit, system, integrated, and validation testing sub-phases. An incident report is used to report problems in the production testing sub-phase. The format will be designed by the test coordinator and will normally contain the information below. Reports will be submitted according to the process established by the Integrated Test Coordinator.

Reported/Updated By:

This is a: [   ] New Problem   [   ] Problem Update

Short Description:

Systems Impacted:

Problem Description:

Action Planned/Taken:

Resolution Assigned To:

Target Resolution Date:

Actual Resolution Date:

PHASE 4 IMPLEMENTATION

Implementation Plan

<u>Master Implementation Plan</u>

Responsibility   ALL COORDINATORS/TEAM LEADERS (Team Plans), IMPLEMENTATION COORDINATOR (Master Plan)

Description   Implementation Planning is the process of documenting the implementation approach and activities for all areas participating in the integration. The Implementation Plan is the script that identifies specifically: what happens; when; who is responsible for making it happen; and who is responsible for validating the completion. It will identify activities from approximately 2 months prior to the conversion through post-conversion support. Within the Implementaion Plan, the following tasks will be included:

85

- Preparation of Last Day/Weekend Procedures, including reporting milestones to the Command Center.
- Identification and distribution of Conversion Task Dependencies List. (attendance at Cross Impact meeting)
- Preparation of a conversion list.
- Preparation and distribution of a hierarchy plan for problem escalation.
- Preparation of a contingency plan in the event of a failed conversion.

Implementation Coordinator Role

An implementation Coordinator will be appointed by the IPO Manager to perform the following functions:
- Develops overall integration scope.
- Consolidates the detailed implementation plans of each work team into a Master Implementation Plan.
- Conducts an implementation dry run with all participants.
- Sets up and staffs an Implementation Command Center in each city participating in the implementation process. Makes arrangements for food and hotel accommodations, as needed.
- Orders and distributes pagers to all implementation participants.

Implementation Plans (Teams)

The Implementation Plan is the checklist for each area of the bank of the tasks needed to be performed to actually implement integration for the period of approximately 2 months prior to conversion through post conversion. Each project group needs to work together to ensure that overlapping tasks are covered. The Implementation Plan will include function name, the identifying activity number, the person(s) responsible for completing the activity, and the date that the activity can start, and should be completed. Since the schedule is also used to monitor the completion of tasks, a column will be added to check that the task is completed on time.

Master Implementation/Communication Plan (Implementation Coordinator)

From a consolidation of the Work Team Implementation Plans and the more detailed Last Day/Weekend Processing Plans, the

86

Implementation Coordinator will prepare a Master Task Plan that will identify responsibilities and dependencies. The Master Plan will include Milestones for reporting to the Command Center. It will also detail Command Center Information, such as location, staffing, hours, phone numbers, voicemail update procedures, and information on recorded status message schedules.

Example:

IMPLEMENTATION PLAN
(Example)

Project Name: **Project number:**
Task: **Prepared by:**
Contact Information for questions:

Activity Number	Project Team	Description of Activity	Responsibility/Dependency	Start Date	End Date	Start Time	End Time	Status

Last Day Processing Procedures

Responsibility   IMPLEMENTATION COORDINATOR (Global Plan), ALL TEAM LEADERS

Description   In all conversions last day processing is extremely critical. Several meetings, under the direction of the Implementation Coordinator, are held to determine last day processing requirements. From these discussions, last day documents are prepared detailing required tasks at ½ hour intervals.

These documents become the guide in detailing all activity that must occur just prior to conversion, and will include checkpoints

along the way. These activities maybe both systematic and procedural. Planning and documenting last day processing requirements is an important step in a successful conversion. Reporting Milestones, as decided in the Last Day processing meetings, should be noted.

The plans and meetings should discuss special branch closing times, last day work flow procedures, and special instructions to Production Control.

Example:

**XXXX BANK INTEGRATION
LAST DAY PROCESSING LIST
(*Example*)**

Project Team: Page Number:
Prepared By: Project Number:
Prepared By: Date:
Approved By: Revision Number:

Note: Reporting Milestones are noted in BOLD lettering.

Activity Number	Project Team	Description of Activity	Assigned To	Start Date	End Date	Start Time	End Time	Depend On	Status

Conversion Weekend Coverage Contact List

Responsibility   IMPLEMENTATION COORDINATOR

Description   This document is used to provide all information necessary to quickly contact anyone needed to participate, or be on call during the actual integration. If Vendor coverage is required, it should be secured well in advance of the integration weekend. The contact list

will contain home, work, and pager numbers. It will also contain general information about the Command Center and Conversion Communications.

COMMAND CENTER(S) CONTACT LIST			
Name	Responsibility	Phone	Schedule

Notes on Conversion Communications:

CONVERSION WEEKEND CONTACT LIST				
Name	Responsibility	Work	Home	Pager

Cross Impacts Documentation & Meeting

Responsibility   OPERATIONS COORDINATOR

Description   This meeting, under the direction of the Operations Coordinator, brings together the various conversion groups of the bank who will be implementing the conversion at or around the same schedule. The primary purpose of this discussion is to identify and communicate the dependency between the various groups (i.e. systems dependency on operations to complete a task before they are able to proceed). This meeting attempts to spell out what is expected, and the time tables related to the conversion. The source of discussion for this meeting will be Implementation Plans, and the more detailed Last Day/Weekend Processing Procedures.

89

Documentation from Teams regarding dependencies will be distributed in order to facilitate correct communication of status and problems over conversion weekend.

Contingency Plan

Responsibility   ALL TEAMS DELIVER TO IMPLEMENTATION COORDINATOR

Description   It is necessary to create a contingency plan in the event that the conversion plan is not able to be executed as scheduled. The probability of needing to use such a contingency plan is low, however it is necessary to know in advance what would have to be done rather than try to develop a plan when time is of essence. The plan must define the steps that would have to be taken to "fall back" to the current processing environment until the conversion can be completed or rescheduled. Each area will have to document the steps that would have to be taken in order to back off some of the conversion steps that may have already been completed. A "Point of No Return" time must be identified as the latest time a decision to abort could be made and still fall back effectively.

Following is a list of some fall back tasks:
- Restore old forms.
- Transcribe Saturday transactions onto old forms.
- Obtain and reformat ATM log.
- Reconnect terminals converted to new systems.
- Cancel temporary help scheduled for post conversion.
- Notify other affected areas.
- Staff for contingency tasks.
- Impacts on customers, operations, etc.

Implementation Weekend Communication Plan

Responsibility   IMPLEMENTATION (SYSTEMS) COORDINATOR

Description   A communication plan will be issued by the IPO Manager specifying who will communicate status, what method will be used, and how frequent the status updates will be. See Example below:

90

Implementation Coordinator

To   IPO Manager
                Coordinators
                Systems and Operations Team Leaders
Frequency:
Format:

IPO Manager

To: Executive Steering Committee Members
                Other Senior Management
                SERVICE COMPANY Management Performance
Group
                Coordinators
Frequency:
Format:

Coordinators

To: Area Management
                IPO Manager
                Group Team Leaders
                Other stakeholders
Frequency:
Format:

PHASE 5- POST IMPLEMENTATION SUPPORT

Post Implementation Support Planning

Post Implementation Support Plan

Post Implementation Support Checklist

Post Implementation Support Checklist Example

Post Implementation Support Phone List

Post Implementation Support Log.

Post Implementation Support Log Example

Post Implementation Problem Log

Post Implementation Support Planning

Responsibility   ALL COORDINATORS/TEAMS

Description   Whenever an implementation takes place, it is essential that support teams are in place to assist employees in handling procedures, customer questions, etc. Although training takes place prior to each implementation, it is impossible to anticipate all of the issues that will arise when the implementation actually takes place. Therefore, it is important to set up support functions like Help Lines to answer employee's questions. Support functions should be staffed by employees who are experienced in, and can answer questions about, a particular product, system procedures, etc. In addition, support planning should involve methods of identifying, reporting, assigning and reporting problems. In short, post conversion support means putting the people, processes, and communication systems in place to minimize customer impacts and impacts on the consolidated organization.

Support coverage

- Customer Service areas must be kept well informed of implementation dates and be prepared with support information to help service customers. Staffing levels should be reviewed

92

and evaluated based on the potential for a large increase in the number of calls.

- Customer notifications are also key sources in aiding post integration support, because they generally explain all anticipated impacts to customers.
- Resource individuals should also be available in the field or support areas to assist employees and customers during the transition (related Team Leaders, trainers, etc.)
- Project Team members provide support in their respective areas.
- XXX staff can assist on-site as support resources for the integrated bank.
- Support for the branches is provided through a Helpline staffed with both Teller and Platform trainers to field phone calls, and to assist in guiding branches through the various implementation issues. It is also helpful to have a Branch Operations employee available as a resource.
- The length of time the Support Services and Helplines are in place will be determined by the number of phone calls, and how employees are adapting to the transition, etc. Generally, the Helpline is in place for 1-2 weeks following integration.
- Product mapping Work Team members and trainers assist with Helpline and/or customer Service areas as the product 'expert', aiding in support of branch and customer inquiries.

Post Support Coordinator Role

A Post Support coordinator maybe named by the IPO Manager. The role maybe filled by the same person named to be the Implementation Coordinator, and the same processes established in the Implementation Process maybe extended to Post Support. The Post Support Coordinator will perform the following functions:

- Sets up and staffs a Post Support Command Center in each city participating in post support.
- Establishes a problem log reporting process with all teams.
- Maintains a Post Support Problem log.
- Notifies coordinators of new and/or open problems that require resolution.

- Conducts daily post support meetings to review previous day's production status an to review open problems.
- Obtains facilities, communications, equipment and supplies for the command center.

Post Implementation Support Plan

Responsibility   POST SUPPORT COORDINATOR (Master Plan), ALL COORDINATORS/WORK TEAM (Individual Plans)

Description   This document provides an outline of the Conversion Support and Communication Plan that will be in effect following conversion. It should be distributed to all affected personnel. A part of the Post Implementation Support Plan will be the Communication Plan for project status.

The Post Implementation Support Plan, in memo format, should state:

- Goals and objectives of the plan. Standard goals are:
- to promptly identify and prioritize post conversion problems or issues
- to determine and implement solutions to problems or issues according to the assigned priorities
- to communicate status
- to insure general support to foster understanding of new processes and procedures.
- Support Coverage Available: Central coordinator, onsite support teams, or technical support teams.
- Status Reporting Requirements/Format/Meeting
- Problem Reporting Hierarchy and Method, including identification, prioritization, resource assignment, and status reporting.
- Anticipated support time periods.

Post Implementation Support Checklist

Responsibility   DEVELOPED BY ALL TEAMS, COMPLETED BY EACH DEPARTMENT

Description   The checklist provides a list of tasks that must be done in an operating or business area each day immediately before and following the conversion.

94

Each department will have its own checklist. There maybe a requirement to return the checklist daily to a central point for monitoring.

The same format maybe used to communicate daily departmental requirements for the period immediately preceding the conversional.

Example:

POST IMPLEMENTATION SUPPORT CHECKLIST
(*Example*)

Department Name: **Prepared by:**
Contact Information for issues/questions: **Preparer Contact Info:**

Description of Activity	Responsibility	Start Date	Deadline	Status

Post Implementation Support Phone List

Responsibility   POST SUPPORT COORDINATOR (For the onsite and Technical Support Teams), COMMUNICATION COORDINATOR (General Departmental Support List)

Description   Two types of phone lists maybe developed for the conversion process:

1. The first required contact list will show the names, phone number, and pager number of the onsite support teams. An integration support team will usually be assigned to each work team.

2. A departmental source guide maybe developed for all employees of the newly integrated bank, with telephone numbers and addresses for various departments throughout XXX. The Guide may list internal departments and services (i.e. Human Resources, Audit, Purchasing), as well as information needed for customer referrals. The guide may provide a moderate level of departmental detail for each functional entry. The guide should also note all

95

"Help" lines that have been created during the integration project to assist particular departments (i.e. Retail, Help Desk). This list will be created by the Communications Work Team.

Post Implementation Support Log

Responsibility   AT THE DISCRETION OF TEAMS

Description   This document is optional within business lines. It is a detailed list of post-conversion issues that surfaced from the onsite support teams. The lists may then be gathered daily by centralized support units for analysis. It is a tool to communicate these issues to management and to serve as a learning device for the next implementation. The log should state all questions handled by the onsite, or centralized support teams, as well as customer contacts regarding the conversion, and therefore will encompass more that may need to be clarified and communicated to appropriate parties. For example, a support area may find that is has handled the same procedural question from many areas. This would indicate that:

1. the procedure may need clarification or modification

2. re-communication maybe necessary

3. follow-up training may need to be scheduled

4. the training process may need to be modified in the future

Example:

POST IMPLEMENTATION SUPPORT LOG
XXXX INTEGRATION PROJECT
(*Example*)

Support Team: **Page:**

Prepared By: **Date:**

Task	Description of Problem	Reported By:	Corrective Action:	Responsibility	Status	Problem Log Entry Y/N?

96

Post Implementation Problem Logs

Responsibility   POST SUPPORT COORDINATOR (Submitted according to the published process).

Description   Each integration project is significantly different, and will encounter some problems. The purpose of the log is to record all systematic or procedural problems encountered during Post Conversion Support. The logs will assign the problems for resolution and track the resolution status. The problem log would not include training issues or procedural "questions". Problems are categorized as Critical, High Priority, or Medium Priority. Problems will be reviewed on an established schedule to ensure that each problem is resolved (see status meetings) and that future conversions do not encounter the same problems.

POST IMPLEMENTATION PROBLEM LOG
XXXX INTEGRATION PROJECT
(*Example*)

#	Priority	Problem	Impact	Resolution	Entry Date	Resolution Date	Current Status

COUSINSGROUP

Project Manager Updates/Status Meetings Schedules

Responsibility   POST SUPPORT COORDINATOR

Description   A post support "Command Center" is setup and staffed to accept possible problem log entries, and to review the prior day's processing status. The Integration Coordinator will hold early AM status meeting conference calls to obtain input as to how the conversion is progressing, and seek to attempt to answer the question "Can we do business today?" PM meetings are also scheduled to review the problem log entries and resolutions. These calls generally last for the first week following conversion weekend.

Attendees of the first week calls include the following:

- IPO Manager
- All Coordinators
- Team Leaders, as decided by Coordinators

Daily broadcasts are also provided via voicemail to a distribution list consisting of a predetermined group of project leaders and member bank management. In addition, broadcasts are also initiated by Coordinators to Team leaders, as needed.

After the first week of conference calls, weekly status reports continue via voicemail distribution for approximately one month following conversion.

Post support plans must be active for the first month following processing.

PHASE 6 – Debriefing review

Deliverables

Post Integration Follow-up List

Repository Consolidation

Review Summary (including problem log review)

Final Plan Review

Review Process

Following each implementation, it is desirable to assess the success of the process in order to improve each subsequent endeavor. In addition, there maybe tasks identified within the conversion that need to be addressed post conversion.

Post Integration Follow-up List

Responsibility   TEAMS/COORDINATORS (For delivery to IPO Manager)

Description   A post-integration Follow-Up List will be completed for activities that must occur post-integration. The Follow-Up List would be divided into two sections:

1. Project related activities that were deemed to be outside the defined scope of the project, but were identified as being necessary in the future.

2. Post conversion clean-up activities.

Each activity should be assigned to an Activity Owner. Clean-up activities would be assigned a completion date. Projects would be scheduled according to the standard XXX Strategic Priorities Process.

100

Example:

Project Related Activities – Out of Scope		
Task Description	**Owner(s)**	**Status**

Conversion Clean-Up Activities		
Task Description	**Owner(s)**	**Scheduled Completion Date**

Repository Consolidation

Responsibility	POST SUPPORT COORDINATOR (Coordinators will deliver Work Team documentation)
Description	In order to keep an accurate record of the integration project activities, the documentation from each work team should be categorized and collected. The Post Support Coordinator will communicate the process for assembling data.

Review Summary (Including Problem Log Review)

Responsibility	IPO MANAGER
Description	At the conclusion of the project, the Director will submit a final narrative report on whether the project plan process successfully

101

COUSINSGROUP

achieved objectives of the project. The purpose of the review is to continually improve the process. The IPO Manager will request specific input from the project participants and sponsors addressing the following items:

- Project Structure and Teamwork
- Project Planning and Control
- Resource Allocation
- Test Scope, approach, and scheduling
- Change Control Process
- Internal and External Communications
- Participation by users and sponsors
- Work plans/Testing/Implementation Plans
- Post Conversion Support
- Training
- Critical Success Factors
- Deliverables
- Problem Logs
- Budget/Savings
- Other strengths and Weaknesses

Recommendations are to be formally documented and distributed to project participants and sponsors for future use.

Final Plan Revisions

Responsibility   TEAMS

Description   Following the final report on the Integration Project, and review of the problem log, it may be necessary for individual Teams to modify their final Detailed Work Plans, Testing Plans, Implementation Plans, or Post Support Plans to incorporate recommendations. Revisions would be required to incorporate missing steps that would improve the process in the future. These revised plans would become part of the Project Repository.

COUSINSGROUP

IPO REPORTING PROCESS AND DELIVERABLES

Deliverables

IPO Action Form Process

IPO Action Form Template

Assumption Process

Assumption Log Template

Issue Reporting Process

XXX Issue Log Template

Project Change Request Process

Change Request Log

Progress Reporting Process

Progress Report Template

IPO Book Executive Summary Template

IPO BOOK Sample

SEE Lotus Notes Data Base

STANDARD XXX PROCESSES

Therese to review as part of the Post Conversion Document as Part of Issues and Recommendations section. Pps 8 - 12

APPENDIX

INDEX LIST NOT UPDATED

www.ingramcontent.com/pod-product-compliance
Lightning Source LLC
Chambersburg PA
CBHW081159180526
45170CB00006B/2141